D0284485

Virginia Woolf Meets Charlie Brown

by

DAVID H. C. READ
Minister of the Madison Avenue Presbyterian Church

William B. Eerdmans Publishing Co.
Grand Rapids, Michigan

Library of Congress Catalog Card Number: 68-28854

Printed in the United States of America

TO PAT

who keeps my feet
on the ground,
my mind open,
and my spirit aloft.

Preface

These are sermons — undisguised. They are also unselected, which means that they represent a year's preaching in a city church, and not a choice by author or publisher of special themes or "those most likely to succeed." They are printed as preached, and offered in the hope that they may be of some help in relating the faith of our fathers to the world of today, and with the conviction that for the Christian preacher to be biblical is to be topical — and vice versa.

—DAVID H. C. READ
New York City

Contents

1. *Our Contact with the Energy of God*

> *... one mightier than I cometh, the latchet of whose shoes I am not worthy to unloose: he shall baptize you with the Holy Ghost and with fire.* LUKE 3:16

The "Confession of 1967" of the United Presbyterian Church closes with the following words: "Now to him who by the power at work within us is able to do far more abundantly than all we ask or think, to him be glory in the church and in Christ Jesus to all generations, forever and ever. Amen."

This is probably the only paragraph in the entire document that was not vigorously questioned and debated, since it is a quotation from the Bible. Some may think of it as the conventional holy noise that is made at the end of a controversial statement or a provocative sermon, to draw the sting of the pious. Yet I believe that this text was deliberately chosen in this instance, since it contains a phrase that is basic to all statements of Christian belief, and to the whole Christian way of life. "The power at work within us" — that's what makes the difference between belief and unbelief, between dynamic Christian living and muddling through on our own.

I have used the phrase "energy of God" in the title of this sermon because this is exactly what "energy" means. It is from the Greek — en-ergy, meaning "working within." The whole question of vital religious belief in the modern world really centers on this decision. Is there, or is there not, in, through, and beyond the secular world as we know it, a divine power, an energy of God, that is available to us all? The skeptic says: No: there are natural powers, the energy of life, the energy of the atom, the energy represented in Einstein's revolutionary formula $E = MC^2$; and there is the energy of the human spirit that increasingly discovers and controls these forces of nature; there is nothing else. The believer says there is something else, something fundamental and decisive — the energy of God which is not only the source of every other energy that is, but the only energy capable of indwelling and transforming the spirit of man. Just as man can, as it were, enter into and control the natural energies of the universe, so we believe that God can enter into and control our human lives and the course of history.

Since you would not be likely to be here unless you believed, or hoped to believe, in the reality of this divine energy, I want to let the Bible speak to us about it. What is a service of worship, after all, unless it brings us into contact with the energy of God? The difference between a merely conventional religious get-together and living worship is defined by the words: "God is spirit; and they that worship him must worship him in spirit and in truth," which could be translated: "God is energy, and they that worship him must worship him with energy and sincerity." In other words, if our spirit is awake, our mind alive, and our purpose sincere, we shall share in the energy of God.

To expound this theme I shall use several Scripture passages, beginning with Samson. This seems to be a quaint old story of a tribal hero who made a matrimonial foray into enemy territory, in the course of which he tore a young lion to pieces. What, you may ask, has this primitive character about whom tall tales were told, got to do with a modern man in search of a God in whom he can believe? All right: the book of Judges is a rough book, and if you want a polite and sophisticated religion you'd better cut it out of your private canon. Let me tell you why I am glad such books are there. It's not only because they contain glorious stories in matchless prose. And it's not only because I want to see the full Bible picture, the development of men's understanding of the divine energy, the Holy Spirit, from the days of the Judges to the final chapters of the Fourth Gospel. It's because the primitive still speaks to the primitive in us. In my understanding of the reality of the Spirit of God I don't always start at the top of the class. There are many today who readily admit that their Christianity is in the rudimentary stage. So let's start with Samson, and see what the story has to say.

This is the wild period in the history of Israel, before the great King Saul brought some order and unity into the tribal free-for-all. Every nation has its wild period, and in that period certain heroes emerge, men of outstanding personality who astonish their fellows by their deeds and leave behind a host of legends of their prowess. My former home had its William Wallace, its Robert Bruce, and its Black Douglas. My present home has its Davy Crockett, its Buffalo Bill, its Daniel Boone, and its Paul Revere. Now we could simply say that the book of Judges is a collection of stories celebrating the early folk heroes of Israel. On one level it is just that. But the Bible always has another level, even in its earliest writings. And here what is injected into the story is nothing less than the energy of God. Similar tales from other sources celebrate the mighty deeds of the hero as if he were some kind of superman. The Bible finds the source of his strength, the vigor of his personality, in a supernatural energy that invades and takes possession. In the moment of crisis — "a young lion roared against him" — we are not told of superman flexing his muscles. What we read is: "The Spirit of the Lord came mightily upon him, and he rent him as he would have rent a kid."

On the primitive level, then, there is the recognition that in the life of a man, or the affairs of a nation, there is a power that defies definition in purely human terms. This power seems to invade and control and provide the extra resources for moments of crisis. Almost every religion and culture has some such belief, but in the Bible the invading power is known as the Spirit of God, and is one with the Creator on whom all things depend. The Spirit of God comes — and a hero does mighty deeds, a king makes wise decisions, a poet breaks into song, a warrior inspires his troops, a prophet rebukes a nation.

At this stage in our understanding this may satisfy, but soon questions arise. Does the Spirit of God only appear intermittently to invigorate his chosen? Does he come as a kind of foreign power sweeping down on the spirit of man, and obliterating his natural faculties? And is this contact with the divine energy a purely arbitrary thing? From some of these stories we may get the impression that the presence of the Spirit is a sporadic and utterly unpredictable occurrence, with no relation to the prayers or longings of the people concerned. In Shakespeare's *Henry the Fourth* the excitable Welshman Glendower makes the claim: "I can call spirits from the vasty deep," to which Hotspur, the cynical Englishman, replies:

> Why so can I, or so can any man;
> But will they come when you do call for them?

That is our question. Granted that the energy of God is a reality in the life of men, is there nothing we can do except wait and hope? Will he come when we do call for him? The answer to this question is not easy, for there is surely an element of unpredictability about the presence of the Spirit of God, and who would like to say that we can summon the divine Spirit to our aid just as we would pick up a telephone and call an ambulance? Yet why should we meet in worship, seeking the presence of God, and why should I talk about contact with his energy, if there is nothing whatever we can say or do that can possibly make any difference?

The answer begins to come as we let the Bible tell us more. And I find that summarized better for us in the fascinating account St. Luke gives of the ministry of John the Baptist.

He begins with a quotation from the prophets:

> *A voice crying aloud in the wilderness,*
> *Prepare a way for the Lord;*
> *Clear a straight path for him.*
> *Every ravine shall be filled in,*
> *And every mountain and hill levelled:*
> *The corners shall be straightened,*
> *And the rough ways made smooth;*
> *And all mankind shall see God's deliverance.*

Why does John take as his text this poem of Isaiah? Surely because it vividly expresses what the prophets had come to believe about our contact with the Spirit of God. They still believed in the divine initiative, but they had come a long way from the naive understanding of the writer of Judges. They proclaimed that the Spirit of God aims at the restoration of all men everywhere to a living contact with the Father in heaven. "All mankind shall see God's deliverance." The energy of God is not the private possession of the chosen few. More than that, they believed that while God alone controls the time and manner of his coming, it is possible for us to be prepared. What a tremendous road-building metaphor Isaiah uses to drive this home! The paths have to be cleared, the valleys filled in, the hills levelled, the corners rounded off, and the rough places smoothed. It's the contractor's prospectus as he plans a superhighway from San Francisco to New York. And the point is surely that if we really want a living contact with the energy of God, there is something to be done. There's a highway to be built into the very citadel of our souls, into the center of a Christian church, into what it is fashionable to call the "power structures" of a community.

What are we doing about this? The plain inference seems to be that if we are totally unconcerned, unwilling to make the slightest move towards preparing ourselves for an influx of God's energy, a new and lively contact with the divine Spirit, then nothing will happen. The real question here is: "How serious are we when we say we want a stronger faith, a contact with God that really grips us and shapes us? Does our desire for such a live religion go as far as to interrupt our normal routine? Are we willing to spend a little longer in prayer — or in meditation about these hills of arrogance that have to be levelled, these valleys of depression that have to be filled up, these rough corners that need to be smoothed? Do we come to worship with any real expectancy that God may have dealings with us in the depths of our being?" When we plan here together to renew our worship, or to alert ourselves to Bible study, or provide opportunities for education and devotion during Lent, we are not pressing a number of buttons by which the Spirit of God may be summoned, but we are most surely attempting "to prepare the way of the Lord." Real contact with the divine energy will come when we are in the place and mood to receive him. "The wind blows where it wills," said Jesus; "you hear the sound of it, but you do not know where it comes from, or where it is going. So with everyone who is born from spirit." Are we in the place where the wind is blowing?

When I spoke previously on the relation between spirit and system I got some feedback which could be summarized as follows: "What about some specifics?" And this was exactly the response to the preaching of John the Baptist. And — let this preacher note — he gave them.

"The people asked him, 'Then what are we to do?'" That's the sixty-shekel question for any preacher. What are we to do? "The people" asked this; so the answer was for everyone. And it came in the form of that practical charity that church budgets call "Missions and Benevolence." "The man with two shirts must share with him who has none, and anyone who has food must do the same." Translate that into your personal response to our appeals for clothing, or your contribution to the budget. Translate that into your vote and influence in such matters as world hunger and foreign aid. This is what the Bible means by "Prepare ye the way of the Lord."

But there were special groups there. The tax-gatherers asked, "Master, what are we to do?" The answer shot back: "Exact no more than the assessment." It could equally be the taxpayers who asked the question, and the answer would have been: "Pay no less than the assessment." In other words, in our business life, to prepare the way of the Lord is to be strictly honest.

Then the soldiers asked, "And what of us?" And the answer was no less precise: "No bullying; no blackmail; make do with your pay." That's the word for any of us in public positions — judges, politicians, policemen, military men, teachers, and ministers. To avoid taking personal advantage from a position of trust — that is to prepare the way of the Lord.

So you see contact with the energy of God is not only a question of a sporadic irruption of divine power in the lives of men. Nor is it only a question of spiritual preparation. The energy of God is not something that we can tap in order to use it for our own purposes. It comes to those whose conscience is at work to clear the way. John had no trouble in putting his finger on some of the "rough places" that had to be made smooth. You and I know what they are in our own lives. The Bible will not let us make a neat dividing line between our worship here in church and our conduct in home and business. It may be that there is a step to be taken in the ordering of our daily life, in our relationships with family and associates, in our attitude to public affairs, before the way is ready for a real contact with the energy of God in prayer and worship.

With this passage we have reached a new stage in our understanding of the energy of God. But we are still, let me remind you, within the limits of the Old Testament. John the Baptist was the last of its prophets. We have still to grasp the supreme revelation of the energy of God, and the truth that can make us Christians. This is as far as we can go with the law and the prophets. The people sensed that as they listened to John. We read that "they were on the tiptoe of expectation, all wondering about John, whether perhaps he was the Messiah," but he spoke out and said to them all, "I baptize you with water; but there is one to come who is mightier than I. I am not fit to unfasten his shoes. He will baptize you with the Holy Spirit and with fire."

What do you make of that? We don't use that kind of language any more, but the import is obvious. One was coming to whom all the law and the prophets had pointed. One was coming who would bring the energy of God into the very center of men's lives. One was coming who would make contact with the living God more than an occasional experience, more than a matter of preparation, more than a sensitive conscience. It would be burning and leaping fire within the soul. It would be a flame of devotion nurtured by a personal encounter with the Son of God. For Christ came as the energy of God concentrated in a human life like ours. Christ came to show what happens when such a life is completely controlled by the Spirit of God. And Christ came to offer this life in sacrifice so that it might be resurrected in every one of us today.

The energy of God in which we believe, and which we seek to find, is not a vague something hovering in the universe and waiting to be tapped by those with special skills. The energy of God has been shined into our hearts in the face of Jesus Christ. It is his love, his purity, his patience, his self-sacrifice, his suffering, his transforming grace. The New Testament makes no distinction between the Holy Spirit, as the energy of God, and the Spirit of Christ. Whoever is willing to let Christ really be master within, yielding the hopes, and the fears of the past, the present and the future to him, *has* the Holy Spirit, the contact with the energy of God. We do not need to think any longer of this divine power as impinging on us from outside, making demands on our conscience. It works from within shaping us into the image of Christ, as a fire that burns unquenchable by any adversity or disaster. We have a long way to go, and, as the apostle warned us: "You must work out your salvation in fear and trembling." But he added immediately: "For it is God who works in you, inspiring both the will and the deed, for his own chosen purpose." Do you believe that is true for you?

2. *The Dignity of Faith*

But the father said to his servants, Bring forth the best robe, and put it on him; and put a ring on his hand, and shoes on his feet.
LUKE 15:22

The neighbors probably said: "Look at him. Dressed like a lord — fancy robe, glittering ring, buckled shoes. So that's what prodigal sons are wearing these days."

This sermon begins as a fashion note on the dress and deportment of the Prodigal Son. I doubt if you have ever paid much attention to this particular aspect of the story. Say "Prodigal Son" and the picture that comes to mind is almost certainly of a half-naked creature grovelling for husks in a field with the swine, or a half-remembered Rembrandt of the father welcoming a ragged, dusty, dishevelled lad by the roadside. That's the one we recognize — the tramp, not the debonnaire figure at the top of the table.

What does it matter? Quite a lot if we are to see ourselves in the Christian terms represented by this boy. The parable was not told for its own sake, but to tell us something about our standing in the sight of the Father God. How many times has the point been made in sermons that the only way to come to the Father is in rags? This is the way of the gospel. The Bible makes it very clear. We cannot storm our way into God's presence in the uniform of our own prestige, or saunter in wearing the immaculate clothing of our superior virtue. We come, like the Prodigal, as beggars. As the hymn says:

Nothing in my hand I bring,
Simply to thy cross I cling;
Naked come to thee for dress,
Helpless look to thee for grace;
Foul I to the fountain fly;
Wash me, Savior, or I die.

So this, we say, is the gospel. This is how we have to think of ourselves. "I know that in me dwelleth no good thing," says St. Paul. Isaiah is even more grim about our status before God: "We are all as an unclean thing, and all our righteousnesses are as filthy rags." The voice of Christ comes in the book of Revelation to the church of the Laodiceans: "Because thou sayest, I am rich, and increased with goods, and have need of nothing; and knowest not that thou art wretched, and miserable, and poor, and blind, and naked: I counsel thee to buy of me gold tried in the fire, and white raiment that thou mayest be clothed." This is indeed how we come as sinners to our God — as beggars, in the rags of the Prodigal. We claim his mercy stripped of all status and prestige — one with all our brethren in acknowledging our need. "Lord, have mercy on us," we say, "Christ have mercy on us." We have nothing to offer but our need.

This is true. But is it the gospel? Surely this is only half the story — and a half gospel is worse than none at all. For what point is there, especially today, in driving home to people like you and me the fact that we have no claim on God, that we are not worthy to be citizens of heaven, that we are not model citizens who deserve the applause of the universe, unless we have something more positive to say? At the moment it looks as though churchmen, novelists, artists, dramatists, and satirists are all uniting to strip mankind of all dignity and self-respect. There seems to be a kind of hard-boiled egghead consensus that Swift's Brobdingnagian was correct when he said: "I cannot but conclude the bulk of your natives to be the most pernicious race of little odious vermin that nature ever suffered to crawl upon the surface of the earth." Do Christians have to concur with this sort of denigration of the human race? Are we to think of ourselves as perpetually clothed in the rags of the Prodigal?

The answer is surely obvious. The parable ends not

with rags but with riches. "But the father said to his servants, Bring forth the best robe, and put it on him; and put a ring on his hand, and shoes on his feet." The whole point of the stripping-down is that we may be clothed with the splendor of the sons of God. Christianity goes even farther than the secular judgment in exposing our nakedness, because the end of the story is the new life, the new being that God confers in Christ. Faith is not just a faculty for seeing more clearly how abysmal is our need: it is the way to recovery of true dignity and self-respect. Has the time not come for the church to talk a little less about the rags and a little more about the robe and the ring and the shoes? This is the gospel — that by faith each one of us is given the dignity of sons and daughters of God, assured of the Father's care, and given eyes to see in every one of our neighbors — whatever their race, or color, or status — another prodigal on whom God sets an infinite value. If the only way into this kingdom is to acknowledge our rags, the only way to live in it with freedom and joy is to be assured that we are clothed in nothing less than the dignity of Christ.

When I talk about the dignity of faith I am not advocating either the arrogance of those who think of themselves as a religious elite, or the stuffiness of those who create the image of Christianity in striped pants. Arrogance and stuffiness come from the self-assumed dignity of pride and pretension. Christian dignity comes simply from the knowledge of whom we serve and to whom we belong. It is part of the humility of the meek who, in our Lord's words, "inherit the earth." It rests not on our achievements, but on the grace of God. The Prodigal knew very well that the dignity of his new clothes was conferred by the Father. But can you imagine that it meant nothing to him as he began his new life? So, the Christian is clothed in baptism with the dignity of Christ, and the life of faith is one of "noblesse oblige." As the hymn says:

Be thou my battleshield, sword for the fight,
Be thou my dignity, thou my delight,
Thou my soul's shelter, Thou my high tower:
Raise thou me heavenward, O power of my power.

What difference will it make to officers and members of the church today if we recapture this sense of the dignity of Christian faith, if we think again of the robes rather than the rags of the Prodigal?

First: *it will make a difference in our Christian witness.* I once heard one of our laymen say in a discussion group that "*witness*" is one of those clerical words used only in the pulpit and that the average man today neither understands it nor thinks of using it. I expect this is true, but I've been unable to find another expression that says what I mean. A witness in a court of law is one who testifies to what he has seen or heard, but everyone by his life and conversation is a witness to what he truly believes. In this sense we can't help being witnesses. A cynic witnesses to his lack of faith either in God or his fellow man. A Communist witnesses to his Marxist convictions. A drunk witnesses to his dependence on the bottle. An athlete witnesses to his devotion to physical fitness. A scientist witnesses to his respect for evidence and truth. Christian witness simply means the impression we make as people who profess that Christ is Lord. It doesn't mean shouting from the housetops that we are devout Christians, or continually intruding our beliefs into our conversation. It means the total effect of our lives, at home, at work, or at play, as evidence of our sincere Christian convictions.

Would you not agree that all of us suffer at times from a kind of timidity, a lack of confidence in our Christian witness? Whether we are students, rubbing shoulders every day with many who ignore or ridicule any profession or practice of Christian faith; or church elders whose business and social contacts are often necessarily with those who rule out religion as a live option today; or whatever our daily life is as church members (or ministers), I think we all know the moments when we have been less than bold in affirming and standing by our Christian convictions. There are times when the sheer weight of non-Christian assumptions and attitudes seems to overwhelm us, and we want to tuck our convictions away for Sundays only.

There is a tendency in some quarters today to adopt a somewhat apologetic attitude. We strive to play down the specifics of the faith, and adapt ourselves to the prevailing secular climate. Recent church literature has leaned over backward in confessing the sins of the Christian and trying to show that our beliefs are, after all, quite palatable for the modern mind. So we are lured into explaining away our faith, as if somehow it wasn't quite intellectually respectable to be a convinced and wholehearted member of the Christian church. Or we may be tempted into the safety of silence when a religious or moral question is being debated.

I am not pleading for a brash and opinionated intrusion of our religious beliefs into our daily contacts — at college, at business, or in the social round. But I am proposing to you a greater confidence in the Lord we represent. It is nothing less than his dignity that is conferred upon us. Can anyone who contemplates the majesty of Christ feel that he must in any way apologize for his faith? And when we consider the massive testimony of the Christian church throughout the ages and across the world today — a theological, intellectual, and moral structure unparalleled in history — should any Christian feel one whit inferior when confronted by the chatter of cynicism and unbelief?

The dignity of faith implies that we need neither fear our Christian convictions, nor inject them anxiously into every situation. There is a quiet confidence that comes to those who know the ultimate authority of the God in whom they trust. I think of David, the young shepherd boy, facing both the mockery of the warriors of Israel and the terrors of Goliath, the champion of the Philistines. To the one he says: "The Lord that delivered me out of the paw of the lion, and out of the paw of the bear, he will deliver me out of the hand of this Philistine." And to the other he said: "Thou comest to me with a sword, and with a spear, and with a shield; but I come to thee in the name of the Lord of hosts, the God of the armies of Israel whom thou hast defied."

I think of St. Paul in the midst of a rioting crowd of his enemies, snatched by the Roman soldiers from the pandemonium and carried shoulder-high into the barracks with shouts of "kill him" ringing in his ears. In such a dangerous and undignified position, how does he behave? "He said to the commandant, 'May I say something to you?' The commandant said, 'So you speak Greek, do you? . . .' Paul replied, 'I am a Jew, a Tarsian from Cilicia, a citizen of no mean city.' " And with the utmost dignity he proceeds to give his witness to Jesus Christ. When he had finished, the violence broke out again, and again St. Paul quietly dominates the scene. Tied to a stake for the lash he said to the centurion, "Can you legally flog a man who is a Roman citizen, and moreover has not been found guilty?" The commandant was sent for and he came and asked Paul, "Tell me, are you a Roman citizen?" "Yes." "It cost me a large sum to acquire this citizenship." Paul said, "But it was mine by birth." The dignity of a citizen of Tarsus, the dignity of a Roman citizen — but above all this same Paul was animated by the dignity of Christian faith. "I am not ashamed," he wrote later, "of the gospel of Christ: for it is the power of God unto salvation to everyone that believeth." Can we not say the same? Is it not time for us to remember with confidence and gratitude that we are marked with the baptism of Christ, and members of the universal church which is his Body?

Then comes another challenge to the churches today. It concerns *the dignity of our Christian worship.* Since I speak more about living worship during the Lenten season, let me just stress this one point now. Any attempt to renew, modify, or make more helpful and attractive our forms of worship today must be governed by a strong sense of the dignity of what we do. That dignity does not reside in the respectability of the congregation or — God forbid! — the self-importance of the ministers, but solely in the God whose glory we celebrate. If we forget that worship is directed to the triune God, Creator, Redeemer, Lord and Giver of Life — and think of it as a kind of religious get-together for mutual encouragement, then there is no limit to the stunts and tricks with which we might experiment to enliven our services and to draw the crowd. There is no reason whatever why worship should not be made more meaningful, why the arts of music, song, painting, and dance should not be more freely used, why experiments should not be made in the expression of our worship in contemporary modes, provided we never lose sight of our chief end, which is "to glorify God and to enjoy him forever."

There is thus an inherent dignity in Christian worship, which can be expressed whatever the tradition to which we belong. An elaborate cathedral service where everything moves with grace and precision can have glorious dignity — or can be hollow pageantry. An informal service in the storefront church can possess the dignity of the Holy Spirit — or can be merely an emotional outburst. So long as we think of church services in secular terms, omitting the dimension of the holy, the sense of the supernatural, they will inevitably lose the dignity of faith, and either degenerate into coy familiarity, or find a spurious dignity in humanistic terms. If you open the Presbyterian hymnal to No. 1, which reads, "All people that on earth do dwell, Sing to the Lord with cheerful voice" — you will find a little note in italics that says "with dignity." Let that be the keynote to our worship. It is not the dignity of the minister, or of the choir, or of the congregation. It is the dignity that is conferred by God on a truly worshipping people.

There is one other aspect of the dignity of faith to which our text speaks with regenerating power. It is *the dignity of Christian self-respect.* How do we really think of ourselves in the presence of God and our fellow men? In rags? Yes: often, and rightly so. We know that our own achievements in the moral life are nothing to boast about. Our place is with the publican who says, "God have mercy on me, a sinner," and not with the Pharisee who says, "Lord, I thank thee I am not as other men." But have we forgotten the robes — the robes with which God has clothed us in Christ? Have we forgotten that our Lord himself assumed that there is a proper self-love when he commanded us to love our neighbors as ourselves? Have we forgotten that when we are united with Christ, God sees his Son in us? "Look, Father, look," we pray at Holy Communion, "on his anointed face, And only look on us as found in him." There is no Christian virtue in a self-hatred that crushes from our minds the knowledge of our redemption. To despise ourselves is to despise the clothing the Father has provided for the

Prodigal, to despise the image of Christ in us. And how can we do that? In men we are to see the reflection of him who went our way through storm and sunshine, through bitterness and isolation, through death itself with the dignity of the Son of God. And this is he with whom we are united in the dignity of faith.

This is what I meant by "noblesse oblige." The nobility of the Christian name that we bear imposes on us a standard of conduct. When we have realized what it is to wear the robes of Christ, to be named by his name, surely a Christian self-respect will keep us from certain habits or practices that we know very well to be inconsistent with the name we bear, and with the dignity that has been conferred upon us.

"Father, I have sinned against heaven and before thee, and am no more worthy to be called thy son." Yes: in our worship and our private prayers that is what we have to say. But ought we not listen again to the whole gospel, the end of the story? "But the father said to his servants, Bring forth the best robe, and put it on him; and put a ring on his hands, and shoes on his feet; and bring hither the fatted calf, and kill it, and let us eat, and be merry; for this my son was dead, and is alive again; he was lost, and is found. And they began to be merry."

3. *God — Infinite Yet Definite*

> *And straightway coming up out of the water, he saw the heavens opened, and the Spirit like a dove descending upon him: And there came a voice from heaven, saying, Thou art my beloved Son, in whom I am well pleased.*
> MARK 1:10-11

In three sentences St. Mark describes an event that was the starting point of a movement that has never stopped — the mission of Jesus Christ in this world. From the moment of his baptism by John in the River Jordan to this moment of worship, the mission of Christ is continuous. Every record tells us that this baptism of Christ was the beginning. He stepped out of the shadows of anonymity that day, about thirty years old. Of his previous thoughts and experience we know virtually nothing. But from this time on he was committed to an engagement with the powers of this world that led through conflict, crucifixion, and resurrection to an expanding mission that will not end until his final triumph. As his body on earth today the Christian church across the globe continues the movement that began this event that St. Mark so tersely describes. So let me read it again in a modern translation:

> It happened at this time that Jesus came from Nazareth in Galilee and was baptized in the Jordan by John. At the moment when he came up out of the water, he saw the heavens torn open and the Spirit, like a dove, descending upon him. And a voice spoke from heaven: "Thou art my Son, my Beloved; on thee my favor rests."

It may be that someone is thinking now: "Already, he's lost me. I can see that Jesus Christ started something, and I think we still need the kind of inspiration he provides. But when you talk about mission, and resurrection, and body of Christ on earth, the cloud comes down. And as for this story of Christ's baptism, it's from another world. The heavens torn open, the dove descending, and the voice from heaven — these phrases may once have meant something, but in my mental picture-gallery they get confused with rockets blasting into space, a voice on the radio, and pigeons in Central Park."

Just because we all have some difficulty in relating to a story like this, I want to stay with it now. And I want to stay with it, not as an historic moment that marks the opening of Christ's mission, nor as material for trying to understand what projected Jesus onto the public scene at that particular moment, but precisely as an event that speaks to our confusion about religion in general, and Christian definitions in particular. In other words, I want simply to think through with you two symbols in the story — the heavens opening, and the voice that says, "Thou art my Son."

Recently I was engaged in a series of television dialogues with representatives of great religions — a Jew, an Eastern Orthodox Christian, a Roman Catholic Christian, and a Moslem. If you add to that a Buddhist and a Hindu you would have a sample of the organized religions that still claim the allegiance of the majority of the human race. In a day of dialogue when these religions are not only talking to one another as never before, but also talking to the secularist and the atheist, we are forced to ask again what religion is, and what these mighty traditions have in common. At the same time we must take account of the growing numbers in modern society who are religious by conviction but detached from any church or institution. The question is: What does the religious man or woman believe that the secularist does not believe?

I know that there is a movement in the Christian church today that is impatient with this question. It is said (I believe, quite rightly) that the gospel is not just another religion, and that we don't persuade people to be

Christians by first proving to them that religion in general is true and good. It is also said (I believe, quite wrongly) that Christianity can be understood and practiced in purely secular terms, and that even belief in God is quite unnecessary. Let me just say that however much the gospel challenges and confounds all religions — including Christianity — the ordinary man is surely right in supposing that the Christian shares with every other religion, named or unnamed, a conviction about the universe and our place in it, that the atheist and secularist flatly denies. He believes that there is a meaning to human life given by that which lies beyond our daily experience, and that there is a directing power in the universe beyond and behind all that is discoverable by science. In other words, he believes in God.

At this point, total confusion sets in. What kind of God? A person, a spirit, a power, a presence, an ultimate concern? Who, or what, are we talking about — and should we be talking at all? All kinds of incantations, definitions, symbols, signs, communications sound in our ears, while in the background we seem to hear the ancient voice of the east, and the via negativa of the mystics: "Not this, not that" — you can't say what he is, only what he isn't. Into our babble of God-talk I seem to hear the word of the psalm which, vigorously interpreted, says: "Shut up! and know that I am God." Isn't this the heart of the matter — that real religion means an awareness of that which is infinitely beyond us — a divine presence that we know, whether vividly or vaguely, and that gives us both a sense of obligation and an inward strength?

"I have immortal longings in me," says Shakespeare's Cleopatra, and these "immortal longings" that are in us all are far more than a selfish desire to go on living beyond this mortal scene. They are the hunger for the infinite, the stretch of the mind and soul towards far horizons. If modern technology means that human ambition is to be limited to the exploration and improvement of the material world, no matter how spectacular the achievements, the human race will have receded rather than advanced. There is a sense in which a savage in the jungle, aware of the unseen world, is wiser than a modern technician who, with all his skills, is blind to the divine presence and minus the dimension of eternity.

It is this divine dimension that is meant by the symbol of the "heavens." And the "heavens opening" is a way of speaking about our moments of awareness, of intuition, of actual experience of the infinite. As I talk with people today, whether they are churchmen or not, I do not get the impression that this kind of experience is vanishing in our secular world, or that it is less frequent, or less valued, than it was in the past. Nobody comes into my study and announces: "Last night, or last week, or years ago, the heavens opened for me," but in the last ten days I have heard from at least four different people statements that amounted to just that. They spoke of this sense of the eternal, of God's presence. It comes in so many different ways — to some very surely, to others just dimly; to some continually, to others only occasionally; to some in a high moment of worship as at Holy Communion, to others by a deathbed, or while looking at a newborn child, or while listening to music or the murmur of the ocean; to some as rebuke, to others as encouragement; to still others as a peace that passes all understanding. This is God — infinite, ineffable, the mystery we cannot touch, yet without which all meaning drains away and the world is but cosmic dust.

Yes: the heavens open today as they have in the past. You know it. And many who never enter a church know it. The underground religion of this age is the experience of the infinite, the ultimate, that comes at these moments when the heavens open. For many this is enough; they instinctively reject any formulation of belief, any organization of religion, any more definite or regular communication with the divine. But others are aware that the real dynamic of religion has always come with something more specific, that the world-transforming faiths have proclaimed a living God who can be really known and served, and that the men and women whom the world has called "saints" have always had a much more specific, positive, warm, and intimate relationship with God.

Let's go back to the banks of the Jordan. "He saw the heavens torn open." Yes: this is a moment when the infinite breaks through. Is this all there is to the story —

one example among thousands of the holy, the numinous, at this sacramental moment when Jesus rises from the water of baptism and the sound of the Baptist's voice fades away across the valley? There is more. St. Mark tells us that "a voice spoke from heaven: 'Thou art my Son, my Beloved; on thee my favor rests.' "

In St. Mark's version this is a personal revelation. The voice is heard by Christ. It is his call. It is a definite sealing in his heart of the Father's love — the awareness, if you like, of his inmost being as *the* Son. "The heavens opening" is one thing; this definite, personal experience is another. It is probably like this that Christ himself told the disciples afterwards what had happened. But St. Matthew, writing later, makes a little change. This time the voice is heard by all: "*This* is my beloved Son, in whom I am well pleased."

This change truly represents what has happened in the church. From Pentecost onward the church's task has been to point to Jesus Christ and to deliver the Father's message: "This is my beloved Son." And here we reach the point where we are challenged by the specific revelation. No longer are we talking about a general sense of the infinite: we are face to face with Jesus Christ, and the infinite becomes definite: "*This,* this Jesus, who is one of you, who knows human life in all its heights and depths, who was to be crucified, dead, and buried, who was to rise again, *this* is my Son."

So it was, you remember, on that other occasion when the heavens opened. With three disciples he was on the hilltop, and the infinite, the holy, broke through with such power that all the evangelists could say was that "he was transfigured before them." The disciples would have been happy to stay there, basking in the sublime, the infinite, the holy. And at that very moment again there comes the voice: "This is my beloved Son: hear him."

The New Testament tells of a God who is not only infinite, but quite definite in his approach to us. It is as though the ultimate and absolute narrows down to meet us where we are in the person of a man like us. "This is my Son." And there are those who can tell you that their vague sense of God, their convictions about the eternal dimension, never became a real and living religion until they met in this way with Jesus Christ and yielded themselves to him. Others still find it hard to let their experience of the infinite, of the heavens opening, be narrowed down to any such definite encounter.

Yet do we not all know the highest, the most sublime things in life are always mediated to us in particular? When the heavens open, and we are aware of a beauty beyond all words, it is not beauty in general that we experience — it is this Parthenon, set there on its solid rock above the blue Mediterranean; it is this one daffodil, this chorale written by this Bach, this poem written by this John Milton. When the heavens open, and we are aware of an immense goodness at the heart of things, it is not goodness in general that we experience — it is this friend who stood by us, this act of generosity, this word of kindness that came in time. We know little of courage as an infinite quality in human life; but we know it in this astronaut strapped in his tiny capsule awaiting the unknown.

So we may surely know this infinite God when he comes close in the human life, the definite, dateable, tangible life of Jesus Christ. "That which was from the beginning, which have heard, which we have seen with our eyes, which we have looked upon, and our hands have handled . . ." says the apostle John, "that which we have seen and heard declare we unto you." This is where Christianity began, and this is how it is nourished and sustained. When, on Jordan's banks, the heavens opened, men did not just note it down as an experience of the divine and go back to their jobs, unmoved and unchanged. They knew that in a quite definite way they had been challenged by their God. For Christ was among them — and the Father's voice said: "This is my Son." From then on those who responded, even in the dimmest way, were Christ's men and women — to be marked by his baptism, and to be part of his mission.

The miracle of Christian worship lies in this confluence of the infinite and the definite. And nowhere does this more dramatically appear than in the sacrament of Holy

Communion. For here we bow before the mystery that words cannot describe and say:

> *Holy, holy, holy, Lord God of hosts;*
> *Heaven and earth are full of thy glory.*
> *Glory be to thee, O Lord Most High.*

Then we reach out our hands and take the most definite, material, particular elements of bread and wine, as we hear his voice say: "*This* is my body," "*This* is my blood." We shall never know in this world all that is meant by God. We shall never be able to map the infinite, or define the eternal. But this we can know — this Jesus; and this we can do — by eating and drinking to be united with him.

4. *Beginning with God*

> *Hear, O Israel: The Lord our God is one Lord: And thou shalt love the Lord thy God with all thine heart, and with all thy soul, and with all thy might.*
>
> DEUTERONOMY 6:4-5

"Let us worship God."

With these words Presbyterian church services traditionally began, and they have been restored in our new order of worship. They indicate that we are about to do something specific and unique. They sound the alert to a waiting people, and — ideally — we come to attention. We are going to do something that is different from all else that occupies us during a busy week, although closely related to it. The words remind us that this is the prime purpose of coming together here. This is the first business of the church. Therefore we don't say: "Let us enjoy some community singing"; "Let us listen to a lecture on theology, or a commentary on current affairs"; or "Let us seek some spiritual comfort"; or "Let us express our longing for a better world." We say: "Let us worship God." Let me remind you that of the vast number of different things a church can and should do, this is the only one that is not also done by other societies or group. Together we worship God. Any church that forgets this — no matter how successful, how popular, how busy — ceases to be a church of Jesus Christ and becomes something else.

What makes the subject of worship unexpectedly exciting at the present moment is the emergence of two apparently contradictory moods in our generation. The first is the quite obvious yearning for an expression of the human spirit that goes far beyond the preoccupation with material success. We have the new tools and toys, but we're beginning to wonder what to do with them. No one is sure any longer that what used to be called progress is really going anywhere. We question the ways in which the stupendous new powers of technology are being used. And ahead looms the spectre of an automated leisure that cannot be filled with an eternity of gadgets. We know we shall need the resources of the spirit. We know that the next exploration must be inward as well as outward. This is why the arts are exploding in all directions, as the human spirit seeks a deeper dimension in which to breathe. This is why those with every material comfort are asking again the old question: Why am I here? This is why there is an openness to religion, to the possibilities of worship in every form from the Quaker silence to the psychedelic "trip." When a friend of mine recently asked a student in a secular university why there was such an unusual enrolment in the department of religion, he got the answer: "Because it's the only place around here where the ultimate issues are raised."

But this revival of a sense of worship, a groping after ultimates, a new recognition of the mystery beyond — which is happening just when the advanced theologians have assured us that modern man is perfectly satisfied with a purely secular world — does not mean what the conventional churchman would like it to mean. There is no sign that the new search for the spirit means a stampede towards the worship services of the church. On the contrary, among many sensitive people today there is a revulsion from any standardized and conventional pattern of worship. It's as if they were saying to us: "I know there's something missing, but I can't find it here. I want to breathe, not to suffocate — and your forms, your ceremonies, your hymns, and your prayers stifle me. And I don't want to worship en masse — especially, if I may say so, your masse."

This is the new worshipper, the member of the great non-church of our day. And I want to take his questions seriously, to try to deal with some of them in later sermons in this series. But let me say now that I believe that the church of today must meet the challenge head on with a reaffirmation of Christian worship in real and vital expression, and not by running away. By running away I refer to the proposals to abandon the institutional church, to soft-pedal the historic faith, and to offer to the new worshipper a secular religion that is shorn of precisely that for which he is looking. When the spirit of worship is awakening in our generation it will be tragic if the churches move in the opposite direction, banishing the mystery, explaining away the divine, and merging with the secular world as little more than pressure groups tinged with religion.

This does not mean that we must cultivate worship as a specialized activity, indulged in by the initiate behind closed doors. We don't pull down the blinds and seek a God in abstraction from the life of the world around us. It's a question, rather, of seeing the temporal concerns of every day more clearly in the light of the eternal; of hearing the sounds of today more acutely because in, and through, and behind them we hear the sound of the ultimate. Listen! The noises come to us from every direction — the noise of traffic on the avenue, the noise of a siren as someone is being sped to a hospital, the noise of a jet swooping off to San Francisco; the noises that are not so immediate but just as real — the rumble of impatience from the deprived in the ghetto, the sigh of the hungry from the lands of famine, the crash of a bomb dropping on a village in Vietnam. Worship does not mean stopping our ears so that we cannot hear. But it does mean that through the noise of a rattling, jolting, exciting world we hear the voice of the ultimate, the call of the world unseen: "Hear, O Israel, the Lord our God is one Lord."

To hear this voice is the beginning of worship. If you ask why I should choose this form of words, this ancient formula from the lore of a Semitic tribe perhaps three thousand years ago, I answer that these words are not only basic to the faith for which we stand but are probably the most dynamic and influential group of words the world has even known. They are, of course, the central creed of Judaism — the Shema, so called from the Hebrew word for "hear." They are the opening words of a synagogue service, and are supposed to be repeated twice a day by every believing Jew. It is this expression of faith that has weathered the fearful storms that have beaten on this people throughout recorded history. These words have, in fact, proved more powerful than all the instruments of human might. Pharaoh is dead. Nebuchadnezzar is dead. Antioches is dead. Titus is dead. Hitler is dead. But still the voice continues in every corner of the world: "Hear, O Israel, the Lord our God is one Lord."

This we may know, but do we realize that these words exploded far beyond the story of the Jewish people? The two strongest religions — estimated to represent nearly half the population of the world — Christianity and Islam — rose from, and rest upon, this same affirmation. Jesus said that our response to the Shema is the "first and great commandment," and Mohammed made his form of it the one and only Moslem creed. The words from the unseen, coming to a people in a way we know not, have proved in fact to have the most decisive effect on that which has been seen — the story of the last two thousand years.

But today? Can our new search for the spiritual dimension, our modern hunger for the ultimate, be met with such a form of words?

"Hear, O Israel!" This is what I mean by "beginning with God." And this is how I see renewal coming for our worship, and an answer being found for the groper after God. The trouble is that in our efforts for what is called "more meaningful worship," or in our search for a creed that makes sense, we tend to start at the other end. We investigate religion. We think about the psychological implications of what we do. We theorize. We compare men's ideas. We seek ceremonies that satisfy our needs. We try to build bridges to the unseen. We look for techniques that will make religion real. But surely if there is a God to be worshipped the very first thing to do is to listen to him. "Hear, O Israel!" "Be still; and know that I am God." Worship is not, after all, a mechanism for reaching some kind of religious satisfaction. It is being there when God reveals himself. It is responding to the voice from the other side. This is why true Christian worship begins by a declaration of God's presence,

God's action, God's Word to us in Christ, and moves from there to our response in the offering of our love and our lives.

"Hear, O Israel: The Lord our God is one Lord." Many today are aware of the difficulty of saying anything about God, of forming any clear ideas about him. And they are suspicious of anything that looks like an attempt to do this, to root our religion in some ancient formula that offers some quite unacceptable picture. What have we to do, as modern men, it is often asked, with this Jehovah, or Yahweh of the Israelites in the desert? But this amazing text offers no such primitive god for our worship. True, he has a name. But the word Yahweh consists of just four Hebrew letters that mean nothing more than I AM THAT I AM, or I WILL BE WHAT I WILL BE. Nothing more is implied than that he *is,* and ever will be. The text, in fact, reads like this in the original: YAHWEH, OUR GOD, YAHWEH, ONE. The importance of the "one" is that the universe is thus declared a uni-verse — and we are not delivered over to the thought of competing powers, some good, some evil, in the world unseen. This God reveals himself as "our God" — and there is no other. For the Christian this means that the qualities we see revealed in Jesus Christ are the qualities that are supreme and ultimate throughout all creation, forever and ever. "Hear, O Israel, the Lord our God is one Lord."

This is the beginning of worship. It is the summons from the Creator Spirit to all mankind. Israel means "people of God" and when Christianity used that title it was with the thought that all mankind are called to be God's people. "Go ye into all the world," said the Lord, "and preach the gospel."

The word is "hear," and not "look." Why? For two fascinating reasons. First, the concept of hearing is less corruptible by idolatry. If the word was "look" Israel would have been tempted to make an image like those of the neighboring deities. It was always hard for other nations to understand this invisible God of the Jews. They were convinced that somewhere, somehow, there must be a form to be seen, an idol to be worshipped. In the year 63 B.C. the Roman general Pompey led an expedition to quell rebellion in Palestine, and led his legions into Jerusalem. We can picture this Roman ascending the steps to the Temple, consumed with curiosity to find out what it was that gave the Jews their fierce and unyielding faith. To the horror of the devout he went beyond the Court of the Gentiles, striding into the inner Temple itself. Surely somewhere here, he must have thought, is the final secret of this strange religion. There it was — the huge hanging curtain protecting the Holy of Holies where only the High Priest could penetrate, and that only once a year. But Pompey was riding the crest of Roman victory and cared nothing for the outcries of a captive people. He must know the secret of these Jews. With an imperious gesture he tore aside the curtain, and entered — the first Gentile ever to reach what seemed the heart of the Jewish faith. And we can imagine that the Temple may then have echoed with raucous laugh. For the secret had been laid bare. There was nothing there! In the inner shrine of Judaism there was nothing to be seen.

Nothing to be seen. But there was something to be heard. And those who have heard it have known a secret beyond the reach of Pompey and the skeptical of all ages. "Hear, O Israel, the Lord our God is one Lord." "He that hath ears to hear, let him hear."

The other reason why hearing, rather than looking, is the beginning of worship is that hearing demands a response. The captain of a ship might conceivably say to a member of the crew: "Look, isn't that a beautiful sunset!" And he would presumably look, and that would be that. But if the words were: "Now hear this!" something very soon would have to happen.

"Hear, O Israel, the Lord our God is one Lord" — so what? "Thou shalt love the Lord thy God with all thine heart, and with all thy soul, and with all thy might."

Here it is — the command to worship. If there is anything less congenial to the mind of the modern Protestant than a command to worship, let me know! Of course, I know that nothing is said here about showing up in a church building at eleven o'clock on a Sunday morning. I know that loving God can be expressed in many other ways than singing hymns, and sharing in prayers. Didn't our Lord say that the second commandment is "like" this one, which means that we love God by loving our neighbor as ourselves? But the command stands. "Thou shalt love the Lord thy God." We have to be honest about this, whether we are churchgoers or not. If we have to any degree heard the voice from the eternal, known what it is to be addressed by the Lord our God, are we really responding with all our heart and soul and might? These are strong words. Wouldn't it be true to say that you tend to love with an occasional thought, a mild enthusiasm, and a vague sense of obligation? Wasn't the teenage girl quite honest when she answered the religious questioner: "Yes: I believe in God, but I'm not crazy about him"?

There seems something odd about a commandment to love. How can we love to order? Well, the Gospels make it clear that loving God takes very practical shape. You remember how the interview that Jesus had with the lawyer went? "How do I get this eternal life?" "Well, what does the law say?" "Thou shalt love the Lord thy God with all thy heart, and with all thy strength, and with all thy mind; and thy neighbor as thyself." "Right! Do that and you've got it." "And who is my neighbor?" Then followed the parable of the Good Samaritan. Surely we can see how to that extent the command to love makes sense. When you see a stranger in need, you can help, or you can pass by. It's as simple as that. But there's even a way in which we can respond to a command to love in a more intimate emotional sense. The more we set ourselves in the presence of one who elicits love the more we shall find it being drawn from us. A man may love his parents but if, as he grows up, he not only leaves the home but ceases to think about them at all, that love will die. Somewhere, though, it may be that a thought of them breaks through. He writes, he visits, and love revives.

Can anyone tell me that we do not need such reminders of the Father-God? that we cannot stimulate our love for him by setting aside times and places for his worship? I am going to speak next about this question of whether or not we need forms and ceremonies, why we should get together with a lot of other people in order to worship

God. Let me say right now, that whatever our view may be about this, there is no question about the command to respond to the God who reveals himself to us. Do you notice how the text switches from the community to the individual? "Hear, O *Israel*" — we are being addressed as a people, as a community, as the family of God. Worship begins as we know that God is talking to the whole human family, and specifically to those who have gathered for his worship. But it then involves each one of us individually. "*Thou* shalt love the Lord thy God." The God who speaks out of the dark mystery, the God who sustains the universe and holds all history in his grasp, the God who speaks to the entire community of mankind, is also the God who wants the love that only you can give.

When I think of a worshipping congregation in a church today I am aware, as you are, of much that is in need of change and refreshment, of much that will say little to the questing spirit from the great non-church. But I am also aware of this: that here, with all our faults and imperfections, our faltering faith and shabby love, is the people of God. And worship springs to life when we begin with God, and are alert to the voice that comes from the deep dimension: "Hear, O Israel, the Lord our God is one Lord." And devotion becomes real as this mysterious God then speaks to each one of us in the recesses of our being: "Thou shalt love the Lord thy God, with all thy heart, and with all thy soul, and with all thy might." We hear much today about the crisis of identity. As was said to me once by a student, "I don't know who I am." Well, this is who we are — members of a family to whom God is speaking, and unique individuals who find our meaning and our purpose in this response of love. We are this child brought to baptism. First comes the assurance of God's love; then we know that we belong to his people; then we hear our own name, our own Christian name; then we begin to love him, as the Bible says, "because he first loved us." If this happens then worship is alive. And where else can we go find just this?

5. *Why All This Ceremony?*

Let all things be done decently and in order.
I CORINTHIANS 14:40

If our question is: "What things shall we do when we come together for worship?" this is practically all the New Testament has to say. No orders of service are prescribed, or even described, in these pages. "Let all be done decently and in order." That's all. But before we ponder the implications of this edict of St. Paul, there's a prior question to be asked. Times have changed. Whereas the first-century Christian in Corinth needed to be told that all things should be done decently and in order, the twentieth-century person wants to ask why anything should be done at all. This is certainly the question of many outside the church who are quite alert to religion, and it is also asked by some who are nominally attached to our churches. Why this emphasis on getting together for worship? What purpose is served by the rites and ceremonies of the church?

Probably all of us have felt this way at some time in our lives. I can remember as an adolescent feeling the attraction of the Christian way of life, the excitement of exploring the thought of God, and at the same time being repelled by the formal worship of the church as I knew it. I could see no point in the palaver of getting ready for church, in sitting with a lot of people I scarcely knew, listening to set readings, prayers that seemed remote from my concerns, and a sermon that might, or might not, hold my attention. As we rose and sat down, sang hymns and gave our offerings, all things were done decently and in order — but they seemed to have little to do with whatever real religion was stirring in my soul. So I sat there thinking how delightful it would be to leap from the gallery where we sat and swing across the church from chandelier to chandelier and land in the chancel indecently and in disorder.

So it is in many minds today. On the one side there is our real belief in God and our desire for a Christian life; on the other there is the form and ceremony of the church. Why this huddling together? Why the institution? Why all these ceremonies?

There is an answer. It is an answer that in the end convinced me as it has convinced probably most of us. But the surprising thing is that no direct answer is given to such questions in the Bible. I could find no passage anywhere on which to base a sermon on the necessity of communal worship — except a rather pointed remark in the Epistle to the Hebrews aimed at the church dropout these days: "We ought to see how each of us may best arouse others to love and active goodness, not staying away from our meetings, as some do . . . ." However, that's not an argument: it's a slap in the eye.

Then I began to see why the Bible says nothing about why there should be communal, and therefore formal, worship of God. The reason is simply that no one in those days would ever raise the question. The silence of the Bible is in fact a tremendous argument in itself. It means that neither in the time of the Old Testament nor in the young Christian church was there any shadow of doubt that faith is much more than an individual relationship to God. Religion is never entirely solitary. The Psalmist might pray, "I will sing of the mercies of the Lord for ever," but soon he was saying, "Blessed is the people that know the joyful sound." He might utter the deep private despair of his heart before God: "As for me, my feet were almost gone; my steps had well-nigh slipped," but soon he was saying: "When I thought to know this, it was too painful for me; until I went into the sanctuary of God; then I understood . . . ." The believer was never on his own. He was incorporated in Israel — the people of God — and his private prayer was always enlarged and supported by the common worship of the Temple. It would never occur to the Israelite that he could cut himself off from the religious community, the people of the covenant, and develop a religion and worship of his own. He knew that his faith was nurtured in the fellowship of Abraham, Isaac, and Jacob, and the people of God. He knew he was intimately bound up in the family that was summoned to worship, "to make a joyful noise unto the Lord," to "serve the Lord with gladness," and "come before his presence with thanksgiving." It was no more possible for him to abstract himself from the community and its ceremonies than it would be for a soldier to refuse the obligations and desciplines of his army and go it alone.

Even the great individualists of the Bible — Jeremiah, Amos, Peter, Paul — never for a moment broke from the community of the faith or abandoned its worship. And surely if there was one supreme individualist, one who more than anyone else who ever lived could claim to have a profound personal relationship with the heavenly Father that needed no supplement from corporate worship, it was Jesus of Nazareth. Yet all the evidence shows that even he was completely identified with the community and its worship. Like the prophets of old he frequently criticized the rituals and practices of contemporary religion, but he never withdrew himself from them. On the contrary he underwent circumcision, instruction in the Law, baptism, and the discipline of synagogue worship. Luke tells us in a significant aside, that "he came to Nazareth, where he had been brought up; and, *as his custom was,* he went into the synagogue on the sabbath day." Almost as soon as he began his own ministry he called twelve disciples, who became the nucleus of the Christian church. From every page of the New Testament it is evident that no one dreamed of being a Christian apart from the church and its worship. This is taken for granted. There are no lone Christians, no isolated believers, in the New Testament. The Christian movement began when "the day of Pentecost was fully come" and "they were all with one accord in one place." Those who thereafter believed were not faced with a choice as to whether they would join a church or not and participate in its worship. The expression is:

"The Lord added to the church daily such as should be saved."

If anyone wants to say: "Forget about how they used to view these matters; we're the enlightened individualists of a new age, and we can surely develop our private religion without being bound by any community and its ceremonies," then I would have to say: "Of course anyone can develop his own religion, but he cannot call it Christianity. And if, in fact, it does begin to look very like Christianity then we must ask: 'Where did you get this thought of God, this ethic, this way of prayer, this inspiration? Was it not, directly or indirectly, from the Christian church?' " (That doesn't necessarily mean some minister, you know, or some official document. The church may have been your mother, a good friend, a Sunday School teacher.) And is it really true that we are less bound together, less members one of another, in this age of interdependence, communications, psychological understanding, common hopes and common fears, than in Biblical times? Just as we are kept alive by the cooperation of our brethren — farmers, merchants, truck-drivers, storekeepers, policemen, so our faith is nourished by the spiritual community which is the church, and our worship expressed and completed by its ceremonies.

The church is not an institution that a Christian has the option of joining. We are members from the moment of baptism. When I say, "I believe in the holy, catholic church," I don't think of a vast ecclesiastical machine that imposes on me a lot of rite and ceremonies that I'd rather do without. I think of people. I think now of one lady who united with a church some years ago. She had no close relatives living, and few friends in this community. Soon after coming here she fell fatally ill with cancer. Almost the last thing she said to me was, "I never knew before what a wonderful thing it is to have the backing of the church," She didn't just mean those who visited her. She meant the realization that in our struggles of life and faith we are not alone. With us is the communion of saints, the holy catholic church.

Our love of God, then, our celebration of Christ will be expressed not only in that "little room" where our Lord said we were to pray alone with the Father. It will mean a coming together. What else can be meant by the remarkable saying of Christ: "Where two or three are gathered together in my name, there am I in the midst of them?" This is why we are here — to know that presence, and together to offer worship in the name of the Father, and of the Son, and of the Holy Spirit.

Now comes the big question — just how can such worship find expression? A congregation is not an aggregation — a set of individual worshippers strung together like beads on a rosary. It is a community, a family of God, in which we merge our praise, our meditation, and our prayers. Therefore there must be an initial humility in our approach. No one can expect a communal service to be framed for him alone. No one should expect every detail of a service to correspond to exactly what he would like. In a service of public worship our own devotions are caught up in something broader and greater, and in the fellowship of the Spirit we learn from one another.

How then shall we go about the business of expressing corporate worship? When you think about it surely it becomes obvious that some kind of ceremony, or ritual, becomes absolutely necessary. Nothing whatever is regularly done by groups of human beings without a pattern of action. We have our rituals for our family meals, for our office management, for the conduct of public meetings, for the exercise of democratic government. Every religious body in the world has a ritual, no matter how informal it may seem to be. There is just no way in which a number of people can do something together without a ceremony. In the Old Testament a great deal of space is given to the ritual of worship. As those whose attempt to read right through the Bible has often come to grief somewhere in the middle of Leviticus will testify, the most minute and detailed instruction is given for the worship of Israel. The question is never whether or not we should have a ritual. It is solely what kind of ritual we are to have, and how we are to prevent its going stale, or becoming so elaborate that it becomes an end in itself.

The first Christians were so excited by the new revelation in Christ, by the freedom and joy they had found in the gospel, that these first gatherings for worship were extremely informal and spontaneous. They observed the ritual of the Lord's Supper and readings from the Bible, and probably the Lord's Prayer. But otherwise the service was what we might call a free-for-all. Anyone who felt so moved would get up and praise God, or tell what he had done for them. No apostle laid down new Levitical rules saying that thus and so must the Christian service proceed. Soon the freedom began to degenerate into license. Those brethren who had the gift of speaking with tongues liked to monopolize the gatherings with frenzied outpourings which no one could understand. Others began to turn the Lord's Supper into a love feast of such riotous proportions that some actually gorged and got drunk at the meetings of the church. This is the situation to which St. Paul addressed himself in Corinth. And this is the force behind his admonition: "Let all things be done decently and in order."

So gradually ceremonies were devised that reduced the chaos of charismatic worship, and the liturgy of the church catholic began to develop. Then, as the centuries passed, the opposite danger became apparent. Ceremonies became all-important. Ritual became a substitute for live religion. And gradually the congregation ceased to be an active, participating family of God, and was often little more than a spectator-group watching a ritual going on in the chancel. By the time of the Reformation the church in the West offered the people a spectacle, a drama, in which they had little part. It was this the Reformers set out to correct. They sought the original simplicities of the New Testament, and they strove to bring the people once more into the center of living worship. So they encouraged lively participation in prayers in the vernacular; they brought hymn singing back into the services; they desired all Christians to partake regularly in the Holy Communion. They had no illusions that worship could proceed without any ceremony at all. They had their liturgies. But they were determined that the point of the ceremonies, the shape of the liturgy, should be the lively participation of a worshipping people. All things were to be done decently and in order, just so that everyone present could share in the wonder and glory of Christian worship.

This, then, is the guideline for Christian worship in our

own day. As Protestants we have to note the irony that while the modern Roman Church is busy making its rituals live, and bringing its people into new participation, we have too often moved in the direction of leaving everything to the clergy and fostering a purely spectator attitude to worship. Our task is to make the ceremonies we use, the liturgy we follow "decently and in order," the vehicle of a lively, sincere, and truly communal worship.

To help us to become alert to the Spirit as modern congregations let me close with three brief points about the ceremonies we use.

1. The first is that the reason for ritual, the reason for doing things "decently and in order," is not that we are to become slaves to a system, but that we may be really free to worship "in spirit and in truth." The point is that real worship only becomes possible when our minds and spirits are freed from distraction as much as possible. And we cannot be so freed if we are always wondering what's going to happen next. C. S. Lewis has these pertinent comments about this: "As long as you notice, and have to count the steps, you are not yet dancing but only learning to dance. A good shoe is a shoe you don't notice. Good reading becomes possible when you do not consciously think about eyes, or light, or print, or spelling. The perfect church service would be one we were almost unaware of; our attention would have been on God." In view of recent changes in the order of worship some of you may sympathize with his further remark, "I can make do with almost any kind of service whatever, if only it will stay put!" We are striving as our forefathers did to find forms of worship that are full of meaning and life for this generation, and when we have such forms, we shall stick with them. Ceremony in the church is not for its own sake; it is simply the stable framework which, when forgotten, lets us concentrate on our Lord.

2. The second point is that all Christian ceremonies must combine what I'm going to call the "vintage" and the "vital." Vintage: I make no apology for the metaphor. Did not our Lord say, "No man having drunk old wine straightway desireth new; for he saith, 'The old is better' "? Our form of worship must always contain

that which is old and unchanging. Such is the water of baptism, the bread and wine of Communion. Such is the repetition of the Lord's Prayer and the saying of the creed. Such are also some of the ancient collects, and the vintage is also preserved, I still believe, through the regular use of the King James Version of Scripture. We are not the first Christians that ever were; we stand in a mighty tradition and that tradition should be reflected in our worship today. But this vintage element in our worship must be balanced by the vital. A church is no museum where we reverently contemplate the past. Every item of our worship must be touched by the Holy Spirit, the Spirit of life, so that it speaks to us, and for us as people of today. To do things decently and in order must not mean putting on a pageant of religious memories; it should mean participation in a living drama in which we respond to the Word of God by the offering of ourselves and our world as we really are today.

3. Granted that ceremonies are inevitable, granted that good ritual can free us for real worship, granted that we balance the vintage and the vital in our worship: there is one final thing that has to be said. Christ is Lord in his church, and we meet to worship God through him. Everything else — forms, ceremonies, rites, hymns, windows, robes, ministers—is his humble servant. "Where two or three are gathered together in my name, there am I in the midst of them." "There am I" — nothing else ultimately matters. Doing things decently and in order is no end in itself. It is road-building, preparing the way of the Lord. The dimension of worship that distinguishes it from any other ceremony is simply the presence of Christ. When we sincerely enter the church to worship — "There am I." When we lift up our hearts in song and in prayer — "There am I." When we open our minds and our lives to the Word of Scripture — "There am I." And sometimes, when all ceremony stops, and there is a silence — a silence like that pregnant pause at the end of a hallelujah chorus before the final chord — we know with a strange certainty that this is why we have come together — "There am I." And with that presence we pass through the church doors for the life of another week.

6. *A Sharing of Strength*

And he commanded the people to sit down on the ground: and he took the seven loaves, and gave thanks, and brake, and gave to his disciples to set before them: and they did set them before the people. MARK 8:6

Let me begin with a story — the Parable of the Obstinate Layman.

There was once a layman who went to talk to a minister about worship. "I come to church," he said, "to get my batteries charged." And the minister began to scold him, and to say: "You shouldn't come to church for what you get out of it, but what you put into it." So the layman listened to a lecture about giving and about the duties of a church member, and then he said: "All you say is very true; but I come to church to get my batteries charged."

Then he went to another minister and said the same thing. Now this minister was an expert in liturgy, and he became very indignant. "Batteries charged? — what nonsense!" And he gave him a long talk about the meaning of every part of the service — processions and confessions, doxologies, and glorias, creeds and candles, vestments and versicles. The layman was very polite and said: "I'm sure you know what you are doing, and it is all very important, but I come to church to get my batteries charged."

Then he went to a third minister who said: "Batteries charged? That's old-fashioned pietism. The only reason to come to church is to be challenged with a sermon on an important issue, and then to go out where the action is. Let me sign you up for a protest march next

Saturday." And the layman turned sadly away saying: "But I come to church to get my batteries charged."

Finally he went to an old and wise minister and said his say. And the old minister listened, and then began to talk. He talked of all kinds of things — about giving, about the meaning of church services, about action — and he read from the Bible, and then he prayed. And the layman went away feeling at last that his batteries were charged — and for the first time he began to ask himself: for what?

The point of the story is, of course, that the obstinate layman was fundamentally right in expecting to receive strength and spiritual refreshment in worship, though wrong in thinking that there is no other reason for coming to church, and no clear consequences of being so recharged.

In our Lenten services we seek to explore the true dimensions of worship both in thought and action. I have tried to speak of those things that are often neglected in our tradition — adoration, participation, the shape of the liturgy — and we have used new forms to deepen our experience of public worship. If you feel, as I do, that we need to expand our understanding and to be jolted out of our religious ruts, you will welcome our "alert to worship" and pray that God will grant us a new vision of what Christian worship can be in our world today. But right now I want to return to the simple fact that worship does indeed offer and provide the inner strength we desperately need. Whether we use the imagery of our ancestors and talk of "the feeding of the sheep," or the idiom of today, "charging our batteries," doesn't really matter. Unless the Bible is completely misleading, unless the gospel is an illusion, when we come together under the ministry of Word and sacrament food is offered for the strengthening of the inner man, something is given and received. There is a line from Milton that haunts any preacher who is tempted to forget this:

The hungry sheep looked up, and were not fed.

What is this story set right in the middle of all four Gospels? It is about feeding, the supplying of strength to a fainting crowd of men, women, and children. And it comes to us in the form of straight narrative. Mark records it as he may have heard Peter tell it. You can almost hear the big fisherman speaking, "I was there!" There was this crowd, three days already out in the wilderness listening to Jesus and asking questions. Their provisions were exhausted, and it was only the Master who thought about their long journey back home and how faint they would be. So, of course, we said: "So what? How can anyone provide all these people with bread in this lonely place?" And he said, "How many loaves have you got?" So he made them all sit down; then he took the seven loaves, and after giving thanks to God, he broke the bread and gave it to us to distribute and we served it out to the people. And I tell you, everyone had enough! Yes: everyone had enough, and there were seven baskets full left over! That's what happened."

When we label this story of the disciples of Jesus a miracle we think we've disposed of it. Those who flatly disbelieve that such a thing could happen either write it off as sheer legend, or treat it as a kind of parable. Those who never question any story in the Bible are just as likely to miss the point, because they think of miracles as ancient marvels to be accepted because God and Christ can do anything, and never ask the question, What does this mean? It is because I want us to reach the inner meaning that I ask you to begin with the story as it stands and try to suspend your prejudgment for or against miracles.

It would be easy for me to skip right over the facts as recorded and talk right now about the spiritual food Christ gives to his worshippers. But there are two good reasons for pausing at this point.

The first is that our modern habit of immediately spiritualizing any incident we find difficult to accept as it stands takes the hard facts out of the gospel, and blurs our image of Christ. If the New Testament tells us anything, it tells of a real Christ, who lived a real life, mixed with real people, ate real bread, and drank real wine. If we dodge the miracle in this story we are not really making it easier to believe in the Christ of the Gospels, for we are cutting out the reality of his compassion for the crowd who were starving, the reality of the bread he provided. We are really saying that Christ didn't care about physical starvation but was only concerned with food for the soul. Yet the whole gospel story contradicts this assumption. It reveals a Christ who himself knew what real hunger was, who cared immensely about the physical sufferings of those around him, and who taught his disciples to pray, "Give us this day our daily bread." This story tells me that he gave real bread to his disciples — and that he commanded them to share this real bread with the whole crowd who were there. And it tells me — at this time we call the One Great Hour of Sharing — that we, his modern disciples, in the U. S. A. who have been given bread in abundance (and how much more!) are commanded to share it — and not just some spiritual food — with the hungry world of today. If we too quickly spiritualize the miracle of the bread, we may be tempted to spiritualize our obligations to feed the really starving of this generation.

The second reason for keeping our minds open is that the author of the miracle is Jesus Christ. After I had lectured on miracles in the Gospels at Lenten schools, I was asked if I only believed in miracles that happened two thousand years ago! The short answer is no — yet with this proviso: I would only expect what we call miracle in association with a unique act of God in our world. I am no more ready than anyone else today to believe in apparently impossible events, but when I am confronted with Jesus Christ — himself the unique miracle of God made man — then I am ready to believe that things beyond our present understanding may have taken place. Once we accept the miracle of the incarnation we may surely believe that the power of God was manifest two thousand years ago in quite astounding ways.

Now as we listen to this story again, prepared to hear what it really has to say, a strange feature begins to emerge. This isn't a miracle in the sense that attention is drawn to a fantastic multiplication of the loaves and fishes. At no point in the story is it said that suddenly the bread began to expand visibly before their eyes and that everyone was struck with amazement. The word miracle is not even used. We are simply told that when Jesus was there, and blessed the bread, there was enough for all. If this is miracle it is hidden miracle. No spotlight falls on a fantastic event, a wonder of wonders, to startle the whole of Galilee and bring the multitudes in adoration to the feet of Jesus of Nazareth. We are just told that when he was there, there was bread enough and to spare. That is all.

This, I believe, is what the story is telling us today. And now we can enter into the rich symbolism of the story. For what happened then is just what has happened ever since each time those who believe in Christ meet with him in the supreme act of worship that he has given to his church.

"He commanded the people to sit down on the ground." There they were, the poor, tired, hungry people of Galilee, brought together "decently and in order," at the command of Christ. And here we are, the confused, anxious, perplexed people of today brought together by the same mysterious Word. "And he took the loaves. . . ." Here we have in front of us the bread that he has given, and it is the same Christ who takes it before our eyes, saying, "This is my body, broken for you."

"And he gave thanks." The Greek word here is our word "Eucharist." "Eucharist" is giving thanks. From early days this word has been attached to the sacrament of the Holy Communion. When we give thanks at this holy table we are following his example of adoration and of praise. This thanksgiving, this Eucharist, is our joining with him in the praise of the Creator God from whom all blessings flow.

"And he brake, and gave to his disciples." This is exactly what we do at our sacrament today. Or rather, we should say, this is what Christ himself is still doing in our midst. "This do, in remembrance of me," were his words at the Last Supper; and we know that it is the Lord himself who ministers to us as the bread is broken.

So this is the miracle: that we, the spiritually hungry, the men and women with our batteries run down, should be brought into touch with the ultimate source of all life and strength and refreshment. We are right there with the disciples on the hillside, and their need is our need.

And in the center is Jesus Christ — "the same yesterday, and today, and forever." He is the strength of God, given for us. And in our worship that strength flows into our weakness, and we are fortified with the bread of his body and the wine of his blood.

Do miracles happen today? This is a miracle that the grace of God, the Lord of all being, should flow into us, the children of time. How fantastically in the two thousand years of the church's life has he multiplied the bread! And how miraculously he feeds us now with the strength we need for our pilgrim path. In this sense, worship is indeed a sharing of strength. We do no more than hold out empty hands to receive the bread. And, as surely as the disciples took that bread from him and were refreshed, so he gives us the strength that our souls are seeking.

This dimension of worship is even more profound than we ever guessed when we sought to recharge the batteries of faith. For you will remember that on the hillside there were seven baskets of bread left over. Did you ever think that when you come to gain the inner strength that is given in worship, and especially in this sacrament, there is always something left over? The strength you get here is not for your satisfaction alone. The strength that is shared by disciples around the table is meant to overflow into the world beyond. The batteries that are charged in our common worship are not for your private use.

I like to think that every piece of bread upon this table that conveys to you the energy of Christ, is multiplied in your life today and tomorrow. Because you have been here today and shared in the strength of Christ, will there not be someone in your home, your place of business, or even far away in the streets of Calcutta or the swamps of Vietnam, who will be stronger in body and spirit because of your worship here this morning? The miracle of multiplication is not a distant wonder, tucked away in the pages of an ancient book. It is the Bread of Life, taken by us today and multiplied across the world by our faith and action. This is worship in a miraculous dimension. For the same Christ who took a few fragments of bread and fed a multitude can take the bread we offer him today and feed not only the hungry hearts that are around this table, but through them the needs of a hungry world. Communion is communicated strength.

7. *Sorrow Into Joy*

And ye now therefore have sorrow: but I will see you again, and your heart shall rejoice, and your joy no man taketh from you.
JOHN 16:22

Some years ago I was sitting in a back pew of a church on a December afternoon. A Christmas pageant was just coming to a close. The church was dark, except for a twinkling tree and a roving spotlight. Around me were fathers, mothers, children, uncles, aunts, cousins, and some curious visitors. In fact, we were all curious; for what we had just seen was not the conventional cast of angels and shepherds but a cross section of modern life — refugees, teen-age gangsters, a married couple breaking up — and the familiar Scripture was mixed with raucous headlines from the latest newspapers. It was into this jarring world of ours that the holy child had come, and as the last lights went out the spotlight fell on a young man of today. Down from the chancel he came, past the silent rows, and out through that door. And there was only one throbbing sound in our ears as he passed. He was singing, "Were you there when they crucified my Lord?"

At that moment I felt very close to the center of Christian worship. For the scene, the movement, the music, the words blended for a timeless minute into that expression of sorrow and joy that is our response to the gospel. This was real. It aroused emotions, but in so doing it spoke to the heart. For that's where joy and sorrow are lodged — whether we are nine or ninety, whether we are brilliant or dull, whether we are rich and powerful or poor and plodding.

Another moment came back to me. I was standing beside a roughly dug grave under the trees on a spring day in West Germany. Into it was lowered a plywood coffin containing the body of a prisoner of war who had died of exhaustion and starvation. The little forest was our church and a few birds our choir. The congregation was six soldiers in dirty battledress. For an anthem we had a whine and a crackle as an allied plane dived and strafed the wood. Then I spoke the words: "I am the Resurrection and the Life, saith the Lord," and suddenly I knew that Jesus Christ was there — the Man of Sorrows and the man of deep and indescribable joy. Again, it was worship — and it was real.

How do we relate such moments, which everyone has known or surely will know, to the ordered weekly services of the church we know? Can we honestly say that regularly when we come to worship our hearts are touched by the divine sorrow and healed by the divine joy? We know, of course, that there is a mood, a moment that cannot be commanded, and that religion must have its routines as well as its bright points of illumination. I have spoken here about the discipline and duty of worship, and the humility that accepts the common forms. But could we not realize more often within these forms the presence that speaks through our sorrow and our joy, and opens up a new dimension of the real? Sometimes we seem to have so sterilized the services of the church that worship flows on as a religious exercise in which we are not wholly engaged as people of flesh and blood. It's up there, rather like (to quote what Matthew Arnold said of Shelley) "a beautiful and ineffectual angel, beating in the void his luminous wings in vain," rather than down here where we laugh and weep.

This may be why a generation is growing up around us that bypasses the church to find its worship in the art galleries, the movie houses, and the discotheque. At its best the cultural explosion of our day is surely revulsion from a secular materialism towards a realm of the spirit where real emotions are engaged. I am not one of those who simply says: "Fine: let our sorrows be released at *Virginia Woolf* or *Marat-Sade,* our joys expressed in folk singing and the best of the Monkees, and the glory of God in the murals of Chagall — and let's forget about the square and standard services of the church." And that is not just because I am a minister, but because I believe in the gospel of Jesus Christ as a unique revelation of the divine sorrow and joy that can touch and transform the human heart, and that therefore the ongoing worship of his church can alert us to a presence that gives meaning to all else. But we have to confess that too often we have dimmed that presence by our formalities, and smothered the gospel in our conventional language and routines.

There is an element in Christian worship that needs to be liberated. It was there from the beginning, making the meeting of Christians something different from any ritual the world had ever known. It is latent in every service where the gospel is declared, and it can renew and enliven the worship of any church today. I'm going to call it the sorrow-into-joy presence of Jesus Christ. If I wanted one word for it I'd use the word "grace" — but in these days of long titles for films and plays nobody understands one simple word any more! Especially, perhaps, that word.

What I'm talking about is very simply stated in the talk of Christ with his disciples presented in the Fourth Gospel.

The crucifixion is only hours away. Judas has already left on his dark mission. On the table are crumbs of bread and a flagon of wine, the remains of the Supper. Real men are there — not ghostly figures with shimmering haloes; frightened men, sorrowful men, anxious men. They have been through too much, and there is more to come. And the Master speaks. "Ye now therefore have sorrow; but I will see you again, and your heart shall rejoice."

It is possible to detach ourselves from this story and view it simply as a testimony to something that happened long ago. The surface meaning of the text is plain enough. The Lord is saying to his followers that they are sorrowful because he is about to be betrayed and executed, but that when they see him alive again they will be joyful. For anyone with some kind of belief in the resurrection this is the plain meaning of the words — and there is really no more to be said. No more to be said — because we have let the cross and the resurrection be tucked away in that dim corner of accepted doctrine that ceases to move us any more. Most of us here believe that around the year 30 A.D. Jesus Christ was crucified, and then, in some way we do not understand, showed himself alive again to his disciples. So, of course, they were sorrowful when he was taken from them; and, of course, they rejoiced when they saw him again. But there is so often a gap between such a cold belief about something that happened long ago, and the sorrows that grip us at this moment, the joys that swoop on us from our modern skies.

"I will see you again." As so often in the Fourth Gospel the very simplest group of words conceals a range of truth that expands through space and time into the profundities of a living faith. "I will see you again." Yes: the words do speak of the moment just ahead when "the same day at evening, being the first day of the week, came Jesus and stood in the midst, and saith unto them, Peace be unto you. And when he had so said he showed unto them his hands and his side. Then were the disciples glad when they saw the Lord." The Gospel writer had this in mind when he recorded the words of our text. He saw them again.

But was there not something more in the mind of any early Christian who read these words? This book was not written by an historian coolly setting down the facts. Those who first read it were not simply being reminded of what had happened in the past, so that they would just say: "Yes: the disciples were sorrowful, but Jesus saw them again, and they rejoiced." The gospel for them was not a kind of memory wedded to a doctrine. It was life. It was the atmosphere they breathed. Sorrow for them wasn't a distant memory of the disciples: it was the agony of their own fears and doubts, the knowledge of their own sins and betrayals. Joy for them was not a word locked up in a book about Jesus: it was what they knew when they came together in his name. So when they met for worship it was a presence that they knew.

The Man of Sorrows and the Man of Joy was really there. And everything they were right then — sad, joyful, anxious, confident, perplexed, hopeful — was caught up and transformed by that presence. "I will see you again."

The world has moved on. And in it, through the rise and fall of empires, the glories and miseries of the human struggle, the expansion of man's control over nature and his fellow man, there has always been a worshipping Christian church. From the catacombs of Rome to the medieval cathedrals to the worldwide network of infinite variety of worship at this moment,

The voice of prayer is never silent,
Nor dies the strain of praise away.

But the power of that prayer, the reality of that praise, depends on the presence. "I will see you again." It is to *our* sorrows and *our* joys that he speaks today. We do not come together just to think of a doctrine: "Suffered under Pontius Pilate, crucified, dead, and buried; he descended into hell; the third day he rose again from the dead." Historical reflection, theological discussion, intellectual inquiry — there is a time and place for all that. The deepest dimension of worship is to be found in this presence — the sorrow-joy presence of the Son of God. And it is not to disembodied minds that he speaks, some brilliant, some dull, some average, but to men and women who meet on the common ground of sorrow and joy. To each one of us in our present experience as flesh-and-blood human beings — always a strange mixture of sorrow and of joy — he comes. And his words are always, "I will see you again."

These words range farther still. For the dimension of worship embraces the eternal. It is not only to our present needs that he speaks, but to that future which is still for frail and sensitive mortal flesh the dark, the unknown, and often the terrifying. "I will see you again." "I, who have been through the dark valley, who have descended into hell, who have been raised from the grave, I will see you again." ("If I go and prepare a place for you, I will come again, and receive you unto myself; that where I am, there ye may be also. And whither I go ye know, and the way ye know.") And, beyond the death of each one of us, as the world moves to that Omega-point where history culminates and the tale is told, the voice of the Son of God speaks through the joy and sorrow of the cosmic story: "I will see you again."

This is what we touch in worship — whether it be the blaze of his glory, or just the hem of his garment. And this presence is not a doctrine to be judged and analyzed, accepted or rejected. His language is not Aramaic, translated into Greek, translated into Elizabethan English, translated into the jargon of today. It is the universal language of the heart — the language of sorrow and of joy. And to those who let down the defenses of formalism, of mental keeping-at-a-distance, of cultivated detachment, he comes.

"Ye now therefore have sorrow." The sorrow we bring to worship ranges from the neurosis of self-pity to the anguish of bereavement or despair. The sorrow we meet in worship has the shape of a cross. That cross tells us that the Son of God was no brief visitant who flashed upon human history to show us the way and tell us how to live. He came to accept the sorrow. He lived with it — the sickness that tortured body and mind, the fears that haunted the imagination, the distress that came with cruelty, accident, and war. It surrounded him, that sorrow, and as he moved to Jerusalem for that final week, it closed in upon him and possessed his soul. When he moved from that upper room to the Garden of Gethsemane it was as though the final and terrible sorrow of humanity was about to crush his spirit. Let us hear the story in a modern version: "When they reached a place called Gethsemane, he said to his disciples, 'Sit here while I pray.' And he took Peter and James and John with him. Horror and dismay came over him, and he said to them, 'My heart is ready to break with grief; stop here, and stay awake.' "

But they didn't stay awake. It was as if their own sorrows could not let them share this immense world-sorrow of the Lord. And into their dreams came the sobbing prayer: "Abba, Father, all things are possible to thee: take this cup away from me. Yet not what I will, but what thou wilt."

What God willed was the gift of his Son, the divine

sacrifice that the mind can never fathom but the believing and grateful heart understands. He was nailed to the cross. And ever since a voice has seemed to sound wherever this cross is held up before men: "Is it nothing to you, all ye that pass by? behold, and see if there be any sorrow like unto my sorrow." But for those who pause to listen and to look there is a quality in this agony that makes it something other than one man's pain, something more than the suffering of the pure in heart. This sorrow draws our sorrows into the heart of God, to be absorbed in a love that is stronger than death. "Surely he hath borne our griefs, and carried our sorrows . . . with his stripes we are healed." This is what moved the poet to write:

See from his head, his hands, his feet,
Sorrow and love flow mingled down;
Did e'er such love and sorrow meet,
Or thorns compose so rich a crown?

This is the Lord who tells us, "I will see you again." So often in our thinking and preaching we have in mind *our* seeing of him, and we reproach ourselves for lacking a true vision of Christ. Many find it hard to conjure up an image of Christ in prayer or in worship. Perhaps we should think again about these words: "*I* will see *you*." He sees us from the cross and knows every sorrow that may be weighing on us now — from the lightest to the heaviest. There is none he does not see and has not already borne. And he sees us from the pure radiance and joy of God, so that every leap of the soul — from sudden laughter to transcendent joy — is an echo of his resurrection presence.

"I will see you again, and your heart shall rejoice, and your joy no man taketh from you." Do you believe that too? This, after all, is the final word: sorrow-into-joy. Where in the secular worship of our day can this assurance be found? The human spirit is indeed finding liberation from the mechanistic universe in a new explosion of art and culture, and the churches are too often prisoners of a drab and dated philistinism. But the church still remains the community where sorrow-into-joy is the divine and liberating Word, where the crucified and risen Lord says to this confused and searching generation, "I will see you again."

Is there any reason why our own response to this presence should not touch the deeper emotions through other channels than the spoken word? Is it not obvious that this dimension of worship demands expression in art and music, in drama, song and dance? The greatest artistic creations of our past have been inspired by the gospel of sorrow-into-joy. I believe that Jesus Christ will "see us again" in this generation in our deepest sorrows and our brightest joys, and that we shall see him, and express our love in a new release of art, a celebration of beauty and of joy.

"Your heart shall rejoice, and your joy no man taketh from you." There are moments when we know what this means. Yet how often we sit detached from the presence, thinking of Christ as someone "out there" about whom we have accepted certain curious beliefs. Yet he is here, seeing us now, right as we are with the sorrows and joys of the present throbbing within us. That cross you see before you speaks of his sorrow that engulfs all sorrow, and its emptiness speaks of the resurrection joy. And he comes, not just through the mind that struggles to know him, but through the pulse of our emotions and opening of the inward eye. "I will see you again." "Even so, come, Lord Jesus."

8. *Where Is God Hiding?*

Behold, I go forward, but he is not there; and backward, but I cannot perceive him: On the left hand, where he doth work, but I cannot behold him; he hideth himself on the right hand, that I cannot see him: But he knoweth the way that I take: when he hath tried me, I shall come forth as gold. JOB 23:8-10

At first sight this may seem a strange text for Palm Sunday morning. We are used to the sound of confidence and triumph, the celebration of God's presence with his people, as his Christ enters the holy city. We make of it a preview of Easter. We decorate our churches; we hear the crowds shouting "Hosanna!" and we sing: "All glory, laud, and honor to thee, Redeemer, King." It's a day when Christians are supposed to express their joyful belief that, in spite of all signs to the contrary, God is in control of his world and Christ is its true and only Lord.

But this, of course, is hindsight. Palm Sunday is a kind of little Easter because we live on the other side of Holy Week, and know what happened. So in retrospect the vision of Christ entering Jerusalem that spring morning is lit by the church with resurrection splendor, and we are invited to join the glad welcome of the cheering crowds. But I believe it may for many today be more helpful to be reminded that the original Palm Sunday was anything but a day of bright simplicity when it was easy to believe in God. The little demonstration of the Galilean pilgrims at the gate of the city just throws into relief a grim picture of desolation and despair. There's an irony in these hosannas, and a terrible emptiness behind the facade of this city sparkling against the blue skies and the Judaean hills. For this is not a moment when God is seen to be in control. This is not a theophany —when God shines through nature and human nature and everybody knows that he is real and near. Rather it is one of those times when the familiar actions of men, and the very beauty of the world around us, instead of conveying God's presence, seem to mock us with his absence. For the average man or woman of Jerusalem, that day God, the God of their fathers, was in hiding while an alien power occupied their land and desecrated their holy places. For the disciples, in spite of a momentary exaltation, God was in hiding as their Master walked into the trap set by his enemies. And for Jesus, more than for anyone else that day, surely it must have seemed that God had withdrawn his presence and left his Son a helpless victim of the malevolence of men and the relentless machinery of their politics.

I want us to see Palm Sunday, not as a distant drama that has become a festival of the church, but as a human situation that raises in an acute form the question that many are asking today: "Where is God hiding?"

It's my guess that most of us here have asked that question in some form in the course of our life. Perhaps someone is asking it right now. You may not come out with it but it lurks in the back of your mind. "I believe in God the Father Almighty" — yet things are happening in our world that surely no almighty Father would tolerate. "Let preachers talk as much as they like about the results of human sin," you say, "and about the educative value of suffering, and about the long-range compensations of heaven; I still wonder what God is doing when men and women are multilated and killed in idiotic accidents, when children are burned in a war they couldn't begin to understand, and when whole nations are swept on collision courses that every sane person wants to avoid." Where indeed is God hiding when those who are trained to trust in him are forced to watch evil forces take command and seem powerless against a tide of hatred and corruption? Where is God hiding when the darkness closes in and I desperately need to know that he is near? For it's just not true that we always realize his presence at the moment of our deepest despair. Where, again, is God hiding at the very moment I'm driven to my knees in prayer? For it's just not true that my quest for a deeper faith is immediately answered by an assurance that he is there.

You will see that I am not talking about the skepticism of those who reject the Christian religion. "Where is God hiding?" is not the question of an atheist — except in sarcasm. I am talking about the doubts and despair of a believer. You don't ask where God is hiding unless basically and normally you believe in him. And one of the surprising ingredients of living faith is precisely this capacity for doubt. For living faith means trust in a living God. It is a personal relationship, and all personal relationships can break down. This is why I find the ideas of the so-called radical theologians so unsatisfactory. People are sometimes shocked because they seem to be doubting so much that used to be believed. The real trouble is that they make real doubt — the kind of doubt that the great saints and teachers of the church have known — quite impossible. For they eliminate the God who can be trusted or doubted in a personal way, and propose some abstraction about which there can be no real problem at all. If you replace the God and Father of Jesus Christ with the thought of "ultimate concern," you can't have doubts any more — for everyone has an ultimate concern. If you replace the conviction that Jesus Christ is a living Lord and Savior with the statement that whether or not there is such a person, this is how you want to live, what is there to have doubts about? If there is no real, living God, but only a great concern in the heart of man, if there is no dimension of the beyond from which our salvation comes, but only an existential illumination of the human spirit, then the agonizing question about God disappears. You've got to have a real God before you can have a real doubt. And that, you know, may be the light at the end of the tunnel for many of us. If you are distressed about the apparent absence of God, your faith is alive. If you allow yourself to be talked out of belief in any real, living God at all you may relieve your religious tensions, but you will have lost the gospel.

"Behold, I go forward, but he is not there; and backward, but I cannot perceive him: On the left hand, where he doth work, but I cannot behold him; he hideth himself on the right hand, that I cannot see him: But he knoweth the way that I take: when he hath tried me, I shall come forth as gold." That sounds like the dark tunnel, doesn't it? The light has gone out and he is groping forward to find someone — but there is nothing. He edges backwards — nothing. His hands go out to the left — no one there; to the right — still nobody. It's the nightmare of being lost and alone somewhere in the subway during a blackout, the symbol of those moods when the isolation of the soul seems absolute and God cannot be found. But such moods pass. The light returns. The presence is known again. What is more devastating is to be out in the bright sunlight of the familiar world, to see everything in its place, to watch the pageant of humanity at work and play, to read the newspapers, walk the streets, to dine with friends, to plan for the years ahead, to think about the years that are past — and find no God. In the tunnel there is an urgency — somewhere, somehow, we must find God. But out in the world of everyday, if God seems hidden, the tragedy is that we may learn to live with the emptiness.

"I go forward, but he is not there." That's the future into which we are peering towards the end of the twentieth century. What lies ahead for humanity? Where are the accelerating currents of history taking us? So much is being presented to our bewildered minds — balance of power, population explosion, cybernetics, revolution, space travel, abundance and leisure, starvation and annihilation. But, in so much of the calculation, so much of the planning, so much of the dreams, "he is not there." What lies ahead for you and me? We make our guess; we take out insurance; we hope for the best. But, so often as we glance into that future, "he is not there."

"Backward, but I cannot perceive him." In our day the floodlights of history roam across the centuries behind us, and brilliant minds try to make some sense of the human story. Information pours in from documents and digs, and the experts offer their views. Is it a consistent tale of progress from the amoeba to Einstein, from the chatter of the ape to the General Assembly of the United Nations? Is it the working out of economic laws, or a cycle of inexorable repetition? Is it the story of the mind's adventure, or the expansion of the human spirit to new levels of awareness? Is it the unrolling of a film that has already been taken, or is it a meaningless succession of events — "one damn thing after another"? If we look back on our own life is there anything like a pattern to be seen? So often, like Job, the answer seems to be, "I cannot perceive him."

"On the left hand . . . ." Suppose we stretch that hand out to the infinitely small, seeking to find the ultimate nature of this mysterious world we inhabit. Is there something ticking there that will explain the what and the why of our existence? Modern man has pierced to the infinitesimal in ways that would astound the author of Job. We learn of the atom. We are told of what goes on within the atom. We strive to understand when the scientist talks of the ultimate energies. We know that we can no longer think of the inner structure of matter as an infinitesimal billiard ball, but we get lost when we read of "waves of probability undulating into nothingness." But we are now conditioned to look inward to the heart of things with the eyes of scientific inquiry, and, as for God, many are ready to say with Job, "I cannot behold him."

"On the right hand . . . ." Suppose the right hand stretches up to the heavens? Again we are in the realm of cool observation and mathematical formulae. We ponder the infinities, and are bemused by the billions of galaxies; but in that ocean of space so often our image of God gets lost. "He hideth himself on the right hand, that I cannot see him."

Forward in time; backward in time; down to the infinitely small; up to the infinitely huge — where is God hiding? Have you noticed that this is not just our problem? It is Job's agony. And it is Jesus' agony as he rides into Jerusalem through the cheering crowds. For where was God hiding in that future that awaited him — that sullen conclave of his enemies, that imperial power that would crush him like a fly, these nails that were already waiting in the barracks to be driven through his hands? Where was God hiding in that rough journey through Galilee to this moment, in that agonizing story of the people of God, bullied and badgered through the centuries, and now prostrate before a pagan conqueror? Where was God hiding behind that smiling sun, and the empty skies beyond the pinnacle of the Temple? Where was God hiding in the recesses of these human hearts, where excitement, hope, fear, greed, love, hate seemed mixed into a brew that spelled his death?

No new problem. So I have no new answer. I just know this: that in every age men and women have stood before the big decision of faith, and so we do today. God never has been an obvious and demonstrable inhabitant of his universe so that we can locate him to everyone's satisfaction. How could he be if he is *God* — and not some idol of our creation? There is a sense in which he must hide from us in the mystery of his being, for how could our finite minds and feeble spirits grasp the infinite Creator and Sustainer of all that is? Yet from him have come to mortal men such signs of his presence as awaken faith in all who are ready to respond. And when that faith is roused the world is transformed, and the presence of God is known in every corner of our lives. Such faith is not a blind adherence to traditional dogma, nor an emotion indulged in spite of the evidence. As in the past, so now, it is a confidence in the hidden God that survives every assault of evil, every desolation of the spirit. It is the personal response we make to a divine person who reveals himself as love.

I have let the skepticism of Job have full weight, so that you can know that this was not a Pollyanna character for whom religion was a piece of cake. Now listen to the astounding words that follow immediately after his complaint: "He knoweth the way that I go: when he hath tried me, I shall come forth as gold."

Faith finds its own answers to its problems. "He knoweth the way that I take." Once we have truly met this God in the depths of the spirit where he reveals himself, we shall know of his presence throughout this world of his creation, and through the dark tunnel where we may sometimes wander. He knows the way we take. The way that lies ahead for humanity, and for you and me, is already lit by his presence. The way behind us we know to be marked by the signs of his presence. The way of our minds into the inmost secrets of matter or the utmost reaches of space is then but the following of the path of his creative wisdom.

Why then this agony on the way? Why the suffering of the questing mind, the bruising of the body and the spirit? No quick and easy answer can ever be given, but faith holds to the ultimate purpose of God's love. "When he hath tried me, I shall come forth as gold." That is the invincible hope that has fortified the company of faith throughout the years. The God who sometimes seems to be hiding never ceases to be at work bringing good out of evil, silently transforming the suffering of those who love him into a spiritual energy that flows through this needy world into life eternal.

All who have chosen the way of faith, today or in the past, know that this is the light by which they live. "He knoweth the way that I take: when he hath tried me, I shall come forth as gold." And when the Christian comes to worship he knows that, after all his excursions into the land of doubt and disbelief, he has returned to the bright center where this truth is most luminous and compelling. In T. S. Eliot's words:

With the drawing of the Lord and the voice of this Calling
We shall not cease from exploration;
And the end of all our exploring
Will be to arrive where we started
And know the place for the first time.

The place for us is Jerusalem and it is God's love and God's calling in Jesus Christ to which we return. Here was everything that seems to make this world a mess — fear, despair, hate, malice, greed, cruelty — and now, even an innocent man could look forward, backward, to the right hand and to the left, and cry out that God was hiding. And indeed, within a few days, the cry rang out from beside these walls: "My God, my God, why hast thou forsaken me?" But was there ever anyone so clearly dominated by the conviction that God was at work in and through the storm of events, and the grim mechanics of evil? In his face, in his actions, in his words, in his silences, throughout Holy Week, we can read one unbroken assurance: "He knoweth the way that I take."

"When he hath tried me . . . ." We are about to commemorate these trials. They are written into human history — the controversy, the betrayal, the agony in the garden, the arrest, the interrogation, the insults, the desertion, the flogging, the crucifixion. If there is any place or time to ask: "Where was God hiding?" it is there and then. The pure Son of God, the incarnation of his love — and this utter degradation and pain. This is where the Christian's faith must return and come to rest. For we know that next Sunday we shall celebrate with the church universal the great act of God that vindicated the trust of Jesus Christ his Son, and of all the company of faith. He was bruised and beaten and killed — and on the third day he "came forth as gold." In this event the hidden God revealed where supremely he is to be found. He is to be found in the worship of the risen Lord, and in the yielding of our hearts and minds to him. When we sing "All glory, laud, and honor to thee, Redeemer, King," we defy the powers of darkness and despair, and take our stand with the company of faith. For we have seen through the darkness to the triumph of God's love.

9. *Easter Exercise*

. . . the darkness is passing away and the true light is already shining. I JOHN 2:8 (RSV)

"The darkness is passing away." It doesn't look like it. Not many journalists would make that judgment in our world today. Not many of us perhaps feel like saying this about our own lives. And — let us remember — even fewer believed it when these words were written. There was not much sign of the darkness passing away as one imperial thug succeeded another on the Roman throne, and the average man's life was "nasty, brutish, and short." I want to tell you that there was one reason only why this man was sure that the darkness was passing away. It was not because he was running for office, or was a congenital optimist, or had taken a trip on some local L. S. D., or had just won the Ephesian lottery. It was simply and solely because he believed that Jesus Christ had risen from the dead. It was an exercise of the Easter faith.

There's no possible doubt about this. Whatever you believe about the resurrection, whatever the man over there in the drugstore believes, whatever modern theologians believe, whatever the Pope believes, whatever Mao-Tsetung believes, the evidence is overwhelming that the men who wrote the New Testament, the men who launched the Christian church, were utterly convinced that the crucified Jesus had been seen again alive. This conviction was the lens through which they looked at the whole of life, their future and the future of mankind. It blazed through every word they spoke, and every line they wrote. So we should begin Easter morning, not with the confusions and uncertainties of our own minds, or some dogmatic statement you may not wish to swallow, but with this bedrock fact: that the men who wrote the book that changed the world, the men who began a movement that has had the greatest impact on the human spirit — not only in religion, but in education, the arts, industry, and science — unanimously believed that Jesus Christ had risen from the dead. Many indeed claimed to be eyewitnesses: "That which we have heard," says this same apostle, "which we have seen with our eyes, which we have looked upon, and our hands have handled . . . that which we have seen and heard declare we unto you."

If we want in our day to reach this conviction that "the darkness is passing away," to have some genuine hope that our human story is not doomed to peter out in futility and despair, we have to reckon with the faith that was in these men. It will not do to say that we'd like to borrow their philosophy but cannot swallow their creed. Their philosophy sprang directly from what they believed about Jesus Christ, and I don't believe it can be sustained without the constant contagion of that faith. That's why we have listened this morning not only to the words of St. Paul celebrating the meaning of the resurrection for all mankind — "as in Adam all die even so in Christ shall all be made alive"; "death is swallowed up in victory" — but also to the factual narrative of St. Mark. When the literal darkness of that night was passing away "very early in the morning the first day of the week, they came unto the sepulchre at the rising of the sun," found the tomb empty and were told that he had risen. The Easter faith has all kinds of implications, but its foundation is the conviction that Jesus Christ, condemned by a real character called Pontius Pilate, and executed on a cross sunk into this solid earth, really came back from the dead and was seen alive by his friends. This is not conceived as a purely spiritual event symbolizing a timeless truth, but as an act, a decisive act of God right in the middle of this secular world.

Well, where are we today? How am I going to listen to the resurrection story here? I can kneel by my bed on Easter morning, shut my eyes tight, and try to transport myself into a different world, the world of "religion" where things are not quite the same as they are in the daily papers, and conjure up an image of a picture-book Jesus rising from the dead. Or I can do what I regularly do — stand by the window overlooking Central Park, and with eyes wide open talk with the God in whom I believe. "This is his world," I say to myself as I look out not only on the grass and the trees, and the banks of cloud, but also on the apartment blocks, the buses, the billboards, and the swings, "and it was in this world that Jesus rose from the dead." Open-eyed prayer is one way of preventing our beliefs from evaporating into some never-never land. God's crucified Son rose from the dead in a place as real as that little mound of grass, and the resurrection is part of that real history of which the most recent chapters are waiting for me to read in today's papers. Therefore I believe that "the darkness is passing away and the true light is already shining."

Only a fool can say that the darkness is past. How can my thoughts and prayers not range out over there to the hospitals where bodies are racked with pain and minds are tormented? Or to the neighbors we do not know? Or to the theatres and art galleries where so much of the spirit's torture finds expression? Or away around the world to Vietnam? No: the darkness is not past, and the shadow of the crucified still falls across the city and the world beyond. But, because I hear again the word that God raised the crucified from the dead, not in some dream-world, but here; and because I awaken to his presence as a contemporary and not as a faded myth, I know that the darkness is passing. The slope of events is to the light. No matter how powerful the forces of the dark may be, their nerve has been cut. They did their worst when Jesus died. There can be no worse to come. For "now is Christ risen from the dead," and "the true light has come." Those who live by this faith are children of the dawn.

It would be easy to rhapsodize about the "children of the dawn" this morning, and satirize the "children of the dusk." We could compare the worship explosion of Easter morning, the chorus of hymns and hallelujahs that fill the churches with the mutterings of our philosophers of doom, the parade of degenerates in novels and plays, and the savage satire that rips the fabric of society apart. But I'm not pleading for a mere revival of old-fashioned optimism, nor am I under the delusion that Christianity is riding the wave of the future. John Updike in a story recently refers to the minority status of the churchgoer in this city. "In Manhattan Christianity is so feeble its future seems before it." He suggests that the churches are back in the struggle of the early Christians. This is what I am talking about — the primitive belief in the resurrection that lit the church of the first centuries and made them really the children of the dawn. I suggest that the time has come to strip down and be more primitive again — in other words, find, and affirm, and live by the primitive conviction that the crucified Savior really rose from the dead.

I'm not asking for a renunciation of our new understandings of the universe, our modern apprehension of the Bible, our experiments in worship, our social applications of the gospel. On the contrary, I believe that the children of the dawn should be more awake to the modern world than the children of the dusk. But I am pleading for a renewal of that primitive faith on which the church was built — that Jesus Christ, who died for our sins, was raised to life in this secular world of ours. Let's be as sophisticated as we like about the details of the story, about our image of God, about the meaning and application of the gospel in modern society, but let's exercise again the leap of faith that responds to the message of the risen Lord. It's that streak of primitive Christianity that will make us truly "children of the dawn," and renew the church in the years ahead. We've had enough of the uncertain trumpets and apostles of confusion. Even the unbelieving world doesn't really expect the Christian church to be among the "children of the dusk." It thinks we should know what we believe.

When we proclaim Jesus Christ as the risen Lord we are committed to the view that the darkness is passing. What is that darkness? Just what it was when the apostle was composing his letter long ago, although we give it other names.

He talked about sin. It was his word for the breakdown in relationships between man and God and between man and man. We call it alienation — the sense of being unable to make contact, being shut up within ourselves, the darkness where we grope for meaning and find no peace. The New Testament shows us Calvary as the place where this alienation, this sin, comes to a fearful climax. It says that Christ, our representative, drew it on himself, and descended into the hell that it creates. There he went down to the deepest darkness the world can ever know, the darkness of despair, alienated from humanity — "despised and rejected of man" — alienated from the Father — "My God, why hast thou forsaken me?" And in that depth "God was in Christ reconciling the world unto himself." How did they know? Why could this not have been simply the final demonstration of the utter absurdity of life? Because on the third day they knew that God had raised him from the dead. Hell had been scoured by God's love, and from then on they could announce: "Sin shall not have dominion over me." And for all who received this news, the darkness was passing away.

The apostles talked about fear. We elongate it to anxiety-neurosis, or dramatize it as "angst." The essence is the same — the terror of the final darkness, the closing in of the black night of the unknown. The resurrection gospel lifted that final fear from the soul of those who believed. They were still, like us, timid people — often afraid, often bewildered. But once their faith responded to the risen Christ, the ultimate fear was gone, for they knew in him the perfect love that casts out fear, the love from which nothing in heaven, or earth, or hell, could ever separate the "children of the dawn." It was not a myth that delivered them but a fact — the rising from the dead of Jesus Christ their Lord.

The apostle talked about evil spirits. We talk about obsessions, mental disturbances, irrational behavior-patterns, collective psychoses. We may not realize to what extent that ancient world seemed peopled by demons, and malignant spirits, or what an exuberant liberation came to the men and women who then heard the story of the resurrection. This was the true secularization of our world, when the resurrection message destroyed this twilight world of evil spirits. But we may also not realize how similar is our plight today when we wrestle with dark powers of evil we can neither control nor understand. We have indeed made strides in dealing with mental disorders, and some progress towards dealing with irrational behavior in individuals. But are there not demonic forces loose in our world — irrational tides of evil that seem to grip communities and nations and cannot be controlled? And don't we need a Christ to worship whose resurrection was the sign that the demons were conquered? Are we too sophisticated to make that leap of faith?

The apostle talked of death. We try not to mention the word, but here our sophistication stops. For death is the leveller. We know infinitely more about the human body and the human mind than the apostle John; but we die just as he did. We talk of our plans to fertilize the earth and colonize the moon, but we die just like our ancestors. We are the generation "come of age" who are reckoned to take charge of events, to decide our future, and to need no God; yet we are as vulnerable as the most superstitious savage. A stray germ, a gangster's knife, a drunken driver — and the most brilliant modern mind is as dead as the caveman. All we have done is to prolong life expectation by a few decades. The punctuation mark remains. Full stop.

But for mankind, whether in the distant past or today, it seldom seems full stop. Rather is it a gigantic question mark. "In that sleep of death what dreams may come?" There are few who are not Hamlets when we face the final question. And the sin, the demons, the fear, are strangely mixed in that contemplation. The world the apostles knew was much obsessed by the great question mark of death, and beneath our sophistication the same unease is lurking. So are we not ready too for the leap of faith that goes out to meet the Word of resurrection?

The plain fact is that the Christian message crashed into the fears and sorrows that were the shadow of death with a shout of triumph. This is not rhetoric, but historic truth. We can hardly conceive today the liberation that was then found in the Easter gospel. The apostles spoke of death, not with a full stop, not with a question mark, but with an exclamation point. "Death is swallowed up in victory!" And this was no sudden access of optimism, or flash of pious hope. Were they not the men who had seen Jesus die? And if he could die, and lie there in a rocky tomb, what hope was there for continued life for the rest of us? The one reason for their astounding reversal of belief, for the exclamation point in their assertion of eternal life, was that they had seen, or heard, that this same Jesus had risen from the dead. Therefore, although the darkness of death continued to descend on them, one by one, they knew that it was the prelude to the world of light. For them, as for all who made this leap of faith, "the darkness was passing away," for the true light was already shining, the light "that shines more and more unto the perfect day."

How about that leap of faith? I talked of an Easter exercise. The trouble is that most of the time we take no exercise in our prayers and worship. We are passive, content to muddle through the valley without lifting our eyes to the hills. But when we do, when something jolts the sleepy soul and we begin to climb towards that peak where the ultimates come into view, then we may find ourselves on the great edge of decision. Shall I opt for a meaningless universe, an empty heaven, a final full stop? Shall I choose to go down fighting as a human spirit protesting the icy indifference of the careless universe? Or shall I make the leap of faith — this faith that responds to the story of the Son of God, crucified and risen from the dead?

All faith is a leap. We trust where we cannot see. This goes for every ultimate conviction, whether religious or irreligious. The leap of faith towards Jesus Christ — which can be sudden and dramatic, or more often slow and almost unnoticed — is a leap in the dark, like any other. But it is a leap *into* light. For as we respond to what is revealed to us of the risen Christ we begin to live in a world where, in spite of all that breaks our hearts, we know that "the darkness is passing away and the true light is already shining."

10. *Is God Over Thirty?*

When Jesus began his work he was about thirty years old. LUKE 3:23

. . . and in a matter of months they heard him say, "It is finished," and he was dead.

Let this be the starting point for our thinking about religion and youth, and perhaps also for a revision of our image of God. Jesus Christ died young. He never reached middle age. Whatever he means to you, this fact has quite startling implications. If you think of him as the supreme teacher of the good life, the wisest man yet to appear on earth, then you are admitting that this wisdom was concentrated in a very young man. If you think of him as the great leader, the example for all mankind, and the one who can guide the nations into the way of peace and fulfillment, you must remember that this is being said about one who was less than half the age of the average chief of state today. If you think of him as one whose life reveals the true nature of the God and Father of us all, then you must believe that God could express all that we need to know of him in a life that barely lasted thirty years. If you hold the full faith of our creeds and confessions and believe that God really became man in Jesus Christ, that the story of his ministry, his cross, and his resurrection is the unique reconciling work of the Father Almighty, then you must believe that all this was accomplished in and through a young man. When he said, "He that hath seen me hath seen the Father," they were not looking at a venerable figure with snowy locks but at one with the physical and mental vigor of youth. What does that do to your image of God?

I begin with this, because in the current debate between youth and age (or, as the older like to say, between youth and experience) there is a tendency to line up religion with the prejudices of the old. Now it may well be that the religion we see on the surface today — the organized network of official church activities — does appear to belong to the older generation, and often indeed to be part of what youth writes off as the "Establishment." Yet Christianity, however it may be molded into the conventions of middle age from time to time, began with a young Savior, young disciples, and a fresh and revolutionary message. And I believe that the gospel never loses in any age its rejuvenating and re-creative power. When we speak of the "revolt" of youth, we should remember that this is precisely how the initial impact of Christ and his followers could be described, and how the effect of the gospel on any of us — whatever our age — could be described today.

What, then, is this youth revolt we are talking about? Whenever I venture to assess what youth is thinking my prayer is that God will somehow prevent me from talking rubbish. And his first answer to my prayer is to remind me that there never has been a period of history when youth and age were in perfect accord.

Said Adam to Eve,
"I begin to perceive
That even young Abel
Whom we raised is unstable:
And now it is plain
We shall have to raise Cain."

You can find all you want about this conflict in the story of Saul and David: the jealousy of age — the old warrior didn't care for the latest song that came floating through the palace windows: "Saul has slain his thousands, but David his tens of thousands"; and later the sulky arrogance of youth as David skulked in the cave of Adullam. This generation didn't invent the generation conflict. It's built in.

I am also reminded not to spin generalizations out of the publicized activities of a segment of our youth. Since vice always is more newsworthy than virtue, and eccentricity than the daily round, the "revolt" of youth can easily conjure up a lurid picture of a whole generation on the loose — black-leathered demons on motorbikes terrorizing a neighborhood, dope-pens where boys and girls with a maximum of hair and a minimum of clothes exchange obscenities, burn draft cards, and thumb their noses at everything their elders hold sacred. That such things happen, that there are perhaps greater excesses of lawlessness in some quarters than ever before, we know to be true. But to judge the youth of the nation on the basis of a section, mostly concentrated in the large cities, is absurd. I have no reason to believe that there is more lawlessness and immorality among the young than the middle-aged, and every reason to believe that there is, on the whole, a healthy, honest, open-minded, inquiring, good-hearted generation coming up behind us.

Wherein, then, lies the revolt? My impression is that the generation gap is somewhat greater now than in the past, and that it is not always easy for one age group to hear what the other is saying. Therefore I want to try to listen very hard to the voice of revolt as it comes from the under-thirties — especially when it concerns the church.

From what I read, from what I hear, and from what I sense, the youth revolt against the churches today takes two main forms. One concerns our public image as an organization, and the other our personal behavior as professed Christians.

(1) The revolt of youth is against what we might call "packaged religion." There are few signs of a revolt against religion as such. On the contrary religion almost ranks with sex as a topic of conversation, and old-fashioned atheism seems definitely out. Students in state-supported colleges where formerly there was often little or no study of the subject are now flocking to courses in religion. When a friend of mine asked one student why, he got the answer, "Because that's the only place round here where ultimate issues are discussed." Concern about religion is, in fact, part of the revolt against a slick, efficient, technological society that is heading very fast towards nobody-knows-what. But a fascination with religion — whether revealed in a reading of Tillich, Buber, and Bonhoeffer, or in a dangerous experimentation with

psychedelic drugs, or the wearing of some outrageous button — is very different from enthusiasm for the church.

The churches seem to appear as the repositories of packaged religion. With their formal services, their organization, their rules, and their rigid posture in society, they look like the very antithesis of what living religion might be. Youth, looking for the expansion of the spirit, the release of the emotions, the enlargement of consciousness that religion ought to mean, is in revolt against the neat wrappings in which we seem to present our beliefs, and the formal channels through which we seem to force the life of the spirit. With their vision of what real contact with God might be they rejected the assembly line by which they seemed to be doomed in the churches to pass from baptism through church school to confirmation and conventional membership in the pattern of their elders.

Let me dramatize this revolt for a moment. A young man stands in the middle of the avenue out there. On one side of him is a conventional church with its notices, its preachers' names, its sermon topics, its lists of activities. On the other side a boutique with a windowful of buttons — some absurd, some witty, some satirical, some political, some religious, some just plain revolting. As he turns his back to the church the buttons become a kind of symbol of his revolt. They are not simply a gesture of defiance, deliberately calculated to shock and annoy an older generation. The religious ones are mixed in with the secular, so that even the most blasphemous indicate an obsession with the question of God. What is being rejected is the church that we know.

If youth tells me that the church is a religious chainstore, run by the Establishment, doling out packaged worship, packaged doctrine, packaged comfort, then I want to listen before I reply. And as I listen I hear the voice of the Hebrew prophets, of Francis of Assisi, of Martin Luther, of John Wesley, of Kierkegaard, and realize that this criticism has to be heard again and again by the church of Christ. We *can* lose the living God in the formula of our creeds; we *can* smother the Spirit in the regularities of our liturgy; we *can* lose the reality of Christian love in the trivialities of our churchiness. The youth revolt reminds us that the church of today is in constant danger of overorganization, of worshipping the ecclesiastical machine rather than the living God.

It is good for us to have this jolt, this apparent rejection of our accepted ways of expressing our religious faith. It is a healthy sign that serious-minded young men and women should question the forms and formulas their elders take for granted. What is not so healthy is the current reaction of the church. For it tends to be either a sheer conservatism that defends the status quo and damns our youth as irreligious and immoral, or else a gutless liberalism that leans over backwards to join the chorus of criticism and pronounce the demise of the churches as we know them. To accept the need of reform, of renewal of a living faith, by no means implies that we are ready to jettison the faith that is the lifeblood of the church or to tear apart the entire structure of her ministry and her worship. We have had enough of these negative critics who snipe at the church from within, and call on us to capitulate to the spirit of the age.

What I would want to say to the youth in revolt against the established churches of our time is something like this: "You are right when you say that we sometimes give the impression of packaging the faith too neatly, and asking you to accept a form of words rather than a living Spirit. But you must remember that the church has a specific Word about God to declare. That Word is Jesus Christ, and wherever he is proclaimed a choice comes to view. He can be accepted or rejected. We don't claim to know all about this Christ, or to interpret him infallibly. But we have been given a gospel that centers on him, and we cannot dissolve it into some vague spirituality that is acceptable to anybody. You are right when you say that we seem to package religion in set forms and ceremonies. But have you noticed that any live movement develops its conformities? Are there not youth groups in our cities where the clothing, the language, the opinions are every bit as conformist in their own way as the average church? You can't damn the church for its conformities unless you believe that religion is a purely private affair. What is needed is the entrance into the church of a youth that accepts the challenge of Christ, and is willing to move from within to reform its structures and make alive its forms and ceremonies. For the God we worship is not a patriarchal figure from the past, but the God of eternal youth.

(2) The personal criticism that youth directs at the church members can be bluntly summarized: it is hypocrisy. It is a hard word, but we must face it. The young are extremely sensitive to the gap that yawns between our professions of belief and our behavior. When they say, "Never trust anyone over thirty," they are referring to the fact that, as we grow older, we tend to a kind of cynical acceptance of this gap — as if we realized that no one can really be expected to live up to all that he professes to believe. Before we resent the accusation — and who doesn't? — let's hear it humbly. They say we talk about love, but act in self-interest; that we sing about peace, but support war; that we shout about moral standards but acquiesce in glaring injustice; that we proclaim the priority of the spiritual, but order our lives by the material; that we condemn youthful promiscuity but practice the serialized polygamy of divorce. All these, and many other charges of hypocrisy are levelled at the conventional over-thirties in our churches.

What are we to say? First, just this: that we have indeed much of which we are ashamed. If we can't say that, we are indeed hypocrites every time we repeat together a confession of sin. We must surely be humble enough to admit that there is not one of us who can claim to be living up to the highest that we know. If we do make such a claim we have never really heard the Christian gospel. For — and this is the next thing that has to be said in all clarity — the Christian church is the place where we come, not to be assured that we are better than our neighbors, but to place ourselves under the judgment and mercy of God. We come to hear such words as these from the thirty-year-old who surely can be trusted: "Alas for you . . . you pay tithes of mint and rue and every garden herb, but have no care for justice and the love of God . . . Alas for you . . . You love the seats of honor in churches and salutations in the marketplace . . . you are like unmarked graves over which men may walk without knowing it . . . Alas for you . . . you have taken away the key of knowledge. You did not go in yourselves, and those who were on their way in, you stopped."

The church, in fact, can be the one place in this world where we are not able to compare ourselves favorably with someone else, because we are forced to compare ourselves with Jesus Christ. It may be true that the older we get the easier it is to dodge the challenge of the gospel, to let the Word of God slip past us as a familiar formula, to acquiesce in a lower level of Christian life than we once aspired to. Here again we need the voice of youth to remind us of what we are really professing to believe.

But I would also ask: is there a mystic barrier at thirty that exempts the younger from any hypocrisy at all? The very charge of hypocrisy, I would remind you, is a dangerous one. It backfires. For which of us is really so omniscient as to be able to know for a fact that his brother is a hypocrite? What do we know of the secret struggles and agonies that go on in someone whom we write off as insincere? At the risk of seeming to flout this warning myself, may I not ask, is there no hypocrisy in the claim that youth has inherited a mess it has not made? in the wholesale condemnation of a society from which so much has been received? in the slick use of slogans like, "Make love, not war"?

While it may be true that the temptations to cold conformity and to hypocrisy tend to increase with age, is it not more true that what matters is, in the end, not calendar years, but the state of the soul? There is no one, whatever his age, who is not prone to the sins and follies we have been talking about. But there is no one, whatever his age, who is not capable of being renewed in spirit, born again, open like a child to the grace of God in Jesus Christ. After all, it is not just to deplore our sins that we come together. It is to rejoice in the rejuvenation of the gospel, the refreshment of the mercies that are "new every morning." In God's presence the differences of age fall away, and all can sing: "Bless the Lord, O my soul: and all that is within me, bless his holy name . . . who satisfied you with good as long as you live so that your youth is renewed like the eagle's."

Is God over thirty? We laugh at the question, and say he is ageless. But in so saying we keep the impression somehow that he must be infinitely old. To be ageless is also to be infinitely young. And it is the youthfulness of God, the modernity of his Spirit, that will in our day, as in the past, revive and renew the church. He sees this family of his now, looking right past the surface of our years, few or many, and we know the truth of the prophetic word: "He giveth power to the faint; and to them that have no might he increaseth strength. Even the youths shall faint and be weary, and the young men shall utterly fall: but they that wait upon the Lord shall renew their strength; they shall mount up with wings as eagles; they shall run, and not be weary; and they shall walk, and not faint."

11. *Virginia Woolf Meets Charlie Brown*

Make no mistake about this: if there is anyone among you who fancies himself wise — wise, I mean, by the standards of this passing age — he must become a fool to gain true wisdom. For the wisdom of this world is folly in God's sight. Scripture says, "He traps the wise in their own cunning".

I CORINTHIANS 3:18-19 (NEB)

We are at worship. That is a Christian activity. There is nothing else like it. When a church becomes alert to its worship all kinds of things begin to happen. Some of these things I have spoken of a few weeks ago. Alert worship means a real sense of God's presence, a confession of real sin and a receiving of real pardon. It means real sacraments and a real hearing of God's Word. But renewal of worship doesn't begin and end in church. It's simply a richer experience every Sunday morning. For true worship spills over into the life of home and business, city and nation. It raises the question of how we're going to live in this complicated world. If we mean what we say and do in the sanctuary, if we really hear the Word of God, then our daily life, our activities, our opinions, our use of time and money will have a different flavor. That's why we are now raising some disturbing questions of our times. Worship is not a hideaway where these things can be forgotten; it is a burning flame where we seek light and fire for the living of this hour.

In that flame we don't find all the answers to the questions that afflict us. There is no quick, clear "Christian answer" to all the controversies and dilemmas we find ourselves involved in. But there is such a thing as a Christian "style of life," a Christian approach, a Christian mood and temper. If there is not, then the New Testament is a most misleading book. For there it is most clearly stated that the Christian is called to a distinctive way of life. In fact, in the early days, Christianity was simply known as "the way." What bothers many of us today is the extent to which this "way," this "style of living" is recognizable in those who are called Christians in our modern world. Would it not be true to say that, while we are willing to make space for the worship and teaching of the church, a great deal of our behavior, our habits of thought, our opinions, at home, at business, and in our social life, are really determined by something else — by what the apostle called "the standards of this passing age"? These standards are often anonymous and undefined, but they press in on us with enormous power. Since we live in the aftermath of two thousand years of Christendom these standards are not obviously pagan, flagrantly unchristian, as they were in St. Paul's time. That's what makes it so easy for us to be unaware that our style of life is often being molded by that which is not Christ. And since most of us want to be considered wise, sensible, sophisticated citizens of goodwill we settle for this secret schizophrenia — being Christians by conviction but letting "the standards of this passing age" determine our views, our daily decisions, and our style of living.

That's why I want to bring before you St. Paul's biting contrast between the wisdom of this world and the foolishness of the Christian. "Make no mistake about this: if there is anyone among you who fancies himself wise — wise, I mean, by the standards of this passing age — he must become a fool to gain true wisdom. For the wisdom of this world is folly in God's sight. Scripture says, 'He traps the wise in their own cunning.' " It's not easy to grasp right away what is being said to us. We're accustomed to hearing from the Bible the praises of wisdom. "Wisdom is the principal thing; therefore get wisdom"; or, even more vigorously, "Go to the ant, thou sluggard; consider her ways, and be wise." Yet here we are told that the secret of the Christian life is foolishness. In fact, two levels of wisdom are being set before us — the wisdom of this world and the true wisdom, God's wisdom, and the path from the one to the other is what he calls foolishness. We're not being offered a passing paradox that occurs to the apostle on his way to more important matters. Everything he has to say to the Corinthians and to us flows from this understanding of the Christian way. "Make no mistake about this," he says, "if there is anyone among you who fancies himself wise . . . he must become a fool to gain true wisdom." I suspect that it is right here — in our grasp of what it means to become a fool — that we are going to learn the secret of the Christian style of living. And it's here that Virginia Woolf meets Charlie Brown.

By a strange twist of literary history *Virginia Woolf* has come to mean for today's public, not the brilliant novelist, but Edward Albee's play, and the movie that shares the title, *Who's Afraid of Virginia Woolf?* That's what I'm talking about—the world of Martha and George, Honey and Nick, the four inebriated intellectuals who hold the stage for three acts of savage self-revelation. And by Charlie Brown, I hardly need to tell you I mean the world inhabited by the hero of Charles Schulz's comic strip "Peanuts" and the somewhat different quartet of Lucy, Linus, Sally, and Schroeder — not to mention the ubiquitous Snoopy.

If you had the stamina you could enter both worlds in the course of one evening, taking in an early performance of *You're a Good Man, Charlie Brown,* then sitting through three hours of *Who's Afraid of Virginia Woolf?* I don't think I'd recommend such a doubleheader — especially on a Saturday night, as I doubt if you would have recovered by eleven a.m. next morning. But I would certainly recommend the experience of both productions. They are, in their own very different ways, reflections of the world we live in, and in content and performance true works of art.

It's not my intention to attempt what you might call a Christian evaluation of either play. Still less, you will notice, am I going to tell you to go and see *Charlie Brown* because it's nice, and stay away from *Virginia Woolf* because it's nasty. Nice and nasty are not words that belong in the vocabulary of Christian criticism anyway. (There's a lot of rubbish that is perfectly nice, and a lot of the Bible that is extremely nasty.) I simply want to let these two plays speak about two worlds that we inhabit, one ruled by what the apostle calls our wisdom — "the standards of this passing world" — and the other by what he calls "the foolishness of God." It's the Virginia Woolf of our cynicism and sophistication that I want to meet the Charlie Brown of our naive bewilderment and crazy hopes.

We meet Martha and George as they arrive home late from a party and proceed to prolong their befuddlement from the bottle. "In vino veritas" — and soon their mutual hates and resentments come savagely at us through the cut and thrust of their devouring dialogue. This is a middle-aged couple in a college community, and soon they are joined by a younger pair — Honey and Nick — against whose relative innocence but equal cynicism the relentless battle is played out. The conversation lays bare with a devastating ferocity the hell into which men and women of intelligence, culture, wit, and worldly wisdom can gradually descend. This is a world of cleverness without compassion, of wit without humor, of passion without values, of fantasy unredeemed by faith. We are exposed to the sophisticated cruelty of the games people play. We are watching civilized human beings indulging in spiritual cannibalism. These are people who know all the answers provided by the wisdom of this world, and with them they are descending into hell — the hell of alienation, lovelessness, hopelessness, and total loss of meaning. Somewhere in the darkness we sense that Martha and George are crying out for each other. Behind the cynicism there is an occasional surge towards the compassion that could redeem them, but in the end the only bond that seems to be left is a mutual fear. "Who's afraid of Virginia Woolf?" says George with his hand on Martha's shoulder. And the answer is, "I am . . . George . . . I am."

We say this is not our world; it is an extreme case of estrangement, and spiritual brutality. So it is; but the fact that it has been written, that it captivates a modern audience, tells us something about the wisdom of our world that we can sense behind the surface calm and rationality. When we come away from such a play saying, "Terrible; disgusting that people should behave like that," are we not a little like the Victorian lady who said to her husband after the curtain had come down on the corpse-strewn stage of the last act of *Hamlet*, "How unlike the home life of our dear Queen!" We know that the world of cynicism, of smooth egotism, of the euphoria of the three-martini lunch, conceals passions and hatreds that can tear men and women apart. And *Virginia Woolf* forces us to ask what saving word there is for us who "fancy ourselves wise . . . by the standards of this passing age."

Well, here comes Charlie Brown. And when I say that, I am not suggesting that all we have to do is to forget the world of alienation and lurking violence and indulge in the happy dream-world of the comic strip. As Robert Short has shown in his book *The Gospel According to Peanuts* this particular strip at least is dealing in its own way with just these problems of our age. Both *Virginia Woolf* and *Charlie Brown* are ultimately theological. The difference is that the one exposes original sin with appalling force and hardly a whisper of redemption, while the other, equally aware of our frailties, is lit by the spark of grace. For Charlie Brown — bewildered, unsure, inquiring, hopeful, put upon, yet courageous — is in many ways the fool that St. Paul is talking about. He is the fool we have to become in order to reach the higher wisdom.

There is a divine simplicity in Charlie Brown, the child of this age. It is not the lazy simplicity of those who dodge the challenge of the modern world, for he is entangled with it from morning to night. He has to deal with the complexities of human relations, the wiles of women, the obstinacy of things, the frustrations of a world of machines (why can't he fly that kite?), and the huge metaphysical problems and the ethical dilemmas of our day. When Sally asks him to forge a letter saying that she must be excused from school as she is needed at home, he launches into an indignant essay on moral theology: "I can't write that! Don't you realize that this is what is wrong with society? This is evasion of responsibility! This is what is eroding our society," only to be met with the smooth rejoinder: "I don't know what you're talking about . . . I'm too young and innocent." So poor Charlie, the truly innocent, learns the hard way how the world will take advantage of his virtues.

Thank God there is a Charlie Brown around in a sophisticated society. We may laugh at him, but perhaps more often we are laughing with him. And the laughter that rises from the audience at the play has a very different quality from that evoked by the cracks in *Virginia Woolf*. It is the laughter that belongs to what I might call the "Christian comedy of life." For when we accept the foolishness of the gospel, when we know something of what it means to receive the kingdom as a little child, when we let the ultimate simplicities come to the surface, something happens to the dark dilemmas, the world of alienation and despair. It's not that we shrug it off with a careless optimism. The Christian fool knows the horror of human sin and suffering. Didn't the Lord Christ take the fool's road to the cross when he could have lived and died as the sage of Galilee? But the Christian fool knows that the final word is resurrection and he sees through the darkness with the eyes of the risen Christ.

Did you see the clown in the film called *The Parable?* Here again is the Christian fool. He does nothing from mere self-interest, but gets himself involved in every trouble and misery he sees around him. He is willing to be taken advantage of, to be laughed at, to do the odd and eccentric thing — for all the time he is moved by the simplicity of love. That loves takes him in the end to a supreme suffering through which new life and hope flows into a world of cruelty and despair.

Isn't our task as Christians today much less a matter of trying to adapt our beliefs to the wisdom of this passing age, much less a matter of adjusting our ethics to the norms around us, than of learning what it means to be fools for Christ's sake? The gospel begins with the foolishness of baptism. What is more absurd than to take a little child of the twenty-first century (for that's when they'll be at maturity) and sprinkle water on him in the name of a Jewish teacher of the first century? And how foolish it must seem for a sophisticated man or woman to dedicate their lives to the service of one whom the wisdom of this world hanged on a cross to die? And how foolish to talk of his being still alive. And how foolish, above all, to take the way of love when self-interest is at stake, to forgive when the instincts cry out for revenge, to be chaste when the world says, "Go ahead: enjoy yourself," to be charitable when we can so delightfully give vent to our prejudices, to be compassionate when it is so much more comfortable not to be involved. Yet all this is part of the way to which we are committed; it is the style of Christian living.

This is the folly that is so needed in the world of *Virginia Woolf*. For in God's eyes it is this empty, ugly, futile wisdom of the world that is the real folly. "Scripture says, 'He traps the wise in their own cunning.'" Isn't that what is happening to George and Martha, Honey and Nick? When Charlie Brown walks in we glimpse something of that Christian foolishness that is the road to the real wisdom.

Is there something you and I can do this coming week that will inject the foolishness of Christ into some area in which we move? There may be a word of forgiveness and understanding to be said, a surprising word of hope where nothing was expected, a gesture of crazy generosity to be made, a new courage to take an unpopular stand. It might be a new experience of prayer, that foolishness the world — and even our own minds — cannot understand. It might simply be the discovery that our own faith is too subtle and complicated, and that it is still possible for us to recover the basic trust in Christ that underlies all our creeds and confessions. For behind all the turmoils and complexities of our daily existence and the agonies of a world that often seems out of control there's a voice that says, "Blessed are the meek: blessed are the merciful: blessed are the pure in heart: blessed are the peace-makers." We don't care who's afraid of Virginia Woolf, if we can hear him say, "You're a good man, Charlie Brown."

12. *On Speaking Out*

> *"Is it right in God's eyes for us to obey you rather than God? Judge for yourselves. We cannot possibly give up speaking of things we have seen and heard."*
>
> ACTS 4:19-20 (NEB)

There was a time when three subjects were taboo in what was called "polite society" — politics, sex, and religion. Now it would appear that if such a ban were imposed, conversation would come to a full stop. We ask: What else is there to talk about except the weather? The first barrier to drop was politics. Since almost everything that concerns our comforts, our cash, our security, and even our existence depends upon political decisions it's absurd not to talk about them; and gradually it has been discovered that Democrats and Republicans can be mixed at the dinner table without risk to the furniture. The next barrier to go was sex — and it went with a crash that can still be heard. For now it seems as though everyone were determined to prove that he could be more outspoken than the next man — or woman. Conversation now runs freely on subjects that used to be reserved for medical journals, and words are used that used to be confined to the men's locker room. Novels reflect an even greater obsession with the subject, and we have come a long way from the time when Edward Gibbon noted about his *Decline and Fall of the Roman Empire:* "My English text is chaste, and all licentious passages are left in the decent obscurity of a learned language" (by which he meant, "The dirty bits are in Latin"). Today anything — but anything — goes in.

The last barrier to fall is religion. Within the last few years there has been an amazing loosening of the inhibitions that used to paralyze religious discussion. Suddenly it seems to have been discovered that there is nothing offensive in raising the ultimate questions with which religion deals, and that it is possible to share beliefs or disbeliefs without feelings being hurt or tempers being lost. Since theology spilled over from the learned journals to the popular press it is not unusual to hear topics such as the Trinity, the ecumenical movement, the "death of God" — or even demythologizing, glossolalia, and apostolic succession — discussed at coffee-tables or cocktail parties. Now that the lid is off people seem more willing to share beliefs or doubts which previously they were embarrassed to mention. The younger the age-group the more likely you are to hear uninhibited discussion of all three subjects — especially religion.

At this point you may want to fling my topic back at me and say: "All right then; speak out! Tell us straight whether you think these changes are good or bad." I'll try to do just that.

In general, I welcome the outspoken generation. I think it good that we can discuss political differences openly and without disguising our opinions for fear of offense. Democracy thrives on this kind of give-and-take, provided it is genuine, tolerant, and reasonably good-tempered. I think it is good that the nineteenth-century conspiracy of silence on sex has been broken, and that young people can learn of their God-given instincts in the open rather than in furtive, sniggering corners. And I think it good that we should be able to share our experiences of life's greatest mystery and most transforming convictions, that we should talk to one another candidly about the beliefs that sustain us, or the doubts that confuse us.

At the same time I have to enter some reservations. There is such a thing as reticence. Fallen man, as depicted in the book of Genesis, has a right to his figleaf. And redeemed man, as portrayed in the New Testament, has still that inner chamber of the soul where he is alone with his God. We are not meant either to wear our hearts on our sleeve or to spill the contents of our mind in all directions without remainder. Our Lord's remark about "casting pearls before swine" can hardly be used by us without arrogance or offense, but surely he was indicating that there is a time for silence and reserve, that there are places where the least said the better. It is especially in the area of sex that this generation seems to be passing well beyond the bounds of legitimate frankness, and seems to betray an obsession that is anything but healthy. When movies are advertised as "bawdy," plays as "tingling with sex," and novels as "frank and outspoken," we have a sick society. At this point I want to speak out against the outspoken.

But — I repeat — the trend to a freer and more honest discussion of the great topics of human life is good. And if it leads to excesses in some areas, then the answer is not a return to a conspiracy of silence, but to a greater outspokenness on the part of those who resent these excesses. In other words, it is time that the silent middle was heard. Political, sexual, and religious extremists speak out loud and clear. It is time for other voices to be heard. And in particular it is surely time for those who believe in God and are committed to the Christian life, to speak out with greater boldness about "the things we have seen and heard."

If you suspect that this sermon is headed towards a plea for a bolder and clearer proclamation of the Christian gospel, you are perfectly right. That's why I chose the Scripture passage that begins with the "boldness" of these "untrained laymen," Peter and John. But before we can talk about the church's speaking out with greater conviction we have to be honest with ourselves. *We* — you and I — are the church, and the amount of conviction in the church's message today depends on the personal persuasion and commitment of her members. So we have to begin with the disturbing question of our own faith, our own working religion, our beliefs and our doubts.

And it is here that I sense the need for some genuine speaking out. A church has its forms of worship, its hymns, prayers, and statements of faith. A visitor dropping in might get the impression that members were all cast from one mold, accepting a set pattern of religion, believing the same things, sharing similar attitudes, and going along with all that is said from the pulpit. Yet nothing is farther from the truth. There is indeed something that draws us together as members of a church, but within that membership there is the utmost diversity of outlook — theological, cultural, political — and a considerable amount of doubt, confusion, questioning, and resistance to what is being said and done. If it were not so this would not be a living church but an ecclesiastical museum. But I have the impression that the hidden ferment of questioning and wondering erupts too seldom in open discussion. The curtain of silence has fallen so that our real beliefs or disbeliefs are seldom voiced. Sometimes church members are afraid to speak out in case they sound too unorthodox in their beliefs, or too disruptive of the atmosphere of smooth agreement that seems to be typical of so-called "middle-of-the-road" churches.

Before we can find a strong, clear voice to speak to our world about "the things we have seen and heard" we need to break through this silence barrier. We need to discuss these things openly and frankly with one another. That's why I welcome the discussion groups and the forum and every contact, in person or by mail, by which church members speak their real convictions and their real confusions. The book of Job always fascinates me as a drama of outspoken conviction and dissent. Listen to the young man Elihu, who has listened long enough to the answers that the conventional representatives of religion were giving to the agonizing Job. It is, if you like, the revolt of youth against the elderly image of mother church with her insufferable wisdom. "It is not the old that are wise, nor the aged that understand what is right. Therefore I say, 'Listen to me; let me also declare my opinion.' " This applies to many more than the young in years. Have you never felt like Elihu? "I also will give my answer; I also will declare my opinion. For I am full of words, and the spirit within me constrains me. Behold, my heart is like wine that has no vent; like new wineskins it is ready to burst. I must speak that I may find relief; I must open my lips and answer."

A living church should be a community where faith is honestly shared, where doubts are openly aired, where all real opinions are charitably heard, and where we learn what it means "to speak the truth in love." Truth — that is what we are reaching when we speak out; love — that is what keeps differences from breeding faction and disruption.

Now let's leave Elihu and turn to Peter and John. I believe that the disciples of Jesus did a lot of speaking out among themselves, and a lot of speaking out in the presence of their Master. It was through an open airing of their real beliefs and their real confusions that they came to their central convictions. But when they had them there was no question whatever about their compulsion to share them with their neighbors. They had something to say, and they spoke out. These were men who had a real experience, a transforming experience of God through Jesus Christ, and they never for a moment thought that this was something to hug to themselves as a private religion. They believed that there was a living God to be known and served, and they believed that the Christ whom they had seen killed on a cross, and then alive again, was the new transforming presence in the world. By the power of the Spirit he transformed their own lives, and they simply wanted to make this presence known. So they spoke about him.

The official religious authorities objected. When Peter, possessed by this transforming power, wrought a cure on a cripple at the Temple Gate, and the disciples became the center of a fascinated crowd, they were arrested and interrogated. " 'By what power,' they asked, 'or by what name have such men as you done this?' Then Peter, filled with the Holy Spirit, answered, 'Rulers of the people and elders, if the question put to us today is about help given to a sick man, and we are asked by what means he was cured, here is the answer: it was by the name of Jesus Christ of Nazareth, whom you crucified, whom God raised from the dead; it is by his name that this man stands before you fit and well!' " The upshot of the trial was that the disciples were ordered "to refrain from all public speaking and teaching in the name of Jesus."

I have often to ask myself what my response would be if some modern authority were ever to impose that ban on me. And what would your reaction be if you were told that continued church attendance could cost you your job or your liberty? I pray that we might have grace to answer like this: "Is it right in God's eyes for us to obey you rather than God? . . . We cannot possibly give up speaking of things we have seen and heard."

This raises at once the question of whether the "things we have seen and heard" in the context of the church are so all-important to us that we could take this stand. And it surely reminds us that the church has lasted through twenty centuries to this day simply because men and women like us have been prepared to speak out about Jesus Christ. Can you imagine that the gospel would ever have reached beyond the walls of Jerusalem, let alone travel around the world, if the apostles had nothing really vital to say? Can you imagine that the authorities would have bothered about them for a moment if all they were doing was discussing the virgin birth or arguing about the Trinity? Suppose their answer to the threat had been: "All right; we'll give up speaking out about Jesus Christ. We're going to have a dialogue."

What I am saying is that if we stand in any sense in the succession of these apostles, we cannot be content simply with the free and open discussion of our problems — important though that truly is. There is still something to be proclaimed. "We cannot possibly give up speaking of things we have seen and heard." Our church has set down what it is that it proclaims, and I want to remind you of it. The purpose, it says, "is to bring men and women into the transforming presence of Christ, in the fellowship of the Spirit, that they may be made over in his likeness; to worship God the Father, and to proclaim the gospel of Christ in word, sacrament and service; and to continue his ministry of compassion and reconciliation both locally and worldwide." Let me fasten on that phrase "the transforming presence of Christ." That is what Peter and John spoke out about. And that is what we must find — new ways to speak to the world around us.

When there is talk today about the church's "speaking out" the reference usually is to taking a stand on some controversy that has moral implications for the Christian. This has to be done from time to time if the gospel is to be really applied and not just left dangling in some spiritual vacuum. And I want to make it perfectly clear that this pulpit is open for any minister or invited guest to declare the Word of God as he sincerely receives it on any question, no matter how controversial. When the apostles and their successors spoke out they seldom met with an enthusiastic and unanimous acceptance of their message.

Yet there is behind all speaking out of this kind a basic and unique conviction to be proclaimed, and in the current upheaval and confusion in the churches it is liable to be forgotten. And that conviction is about the transforming presence of Christ.

This is, after all, something we have seen and heard. We have seen it not just by a backward glance over the astonishing history of the church, but in the lives we have known that have reflected this transforming power. We have heard it, not only in the Word that speaks in the New Testament, but in the language of people like ourselves — a chance word, perhaps, that changed the course of our lives. I would not stand in the pulpit, and you would not sit in the pew, except for something that we have seen and heard. And that something is the transforming presence of Christ mediated to us by the word, the action of another human being.

It is time to talk more, and perhaps to talk differently, of that luminous center by which a Christian lives. By all means let us break the silence barrier and voice our difficulties with the conventional language of the church. By all means let us talk about the agonizing questions of our day. By all means let us break out of the network of tired words and stale ceremonies in which we imprison the gospel. By all means let us listen to the voice of the scientist, the artist, the psychologist, the religion that is different from ours. But there is a Word we have been given, and that Word is Christ. He is both what Eliot called "the still point of the turning world," and the transforming presence that disturbs and renews the whole of life.

Thus I would speak out in a world of doubt and confusion and say that in Christ I find a God who is alive with an eternal youth. I would speak out in a world of skepticism and much despair and say that in Christ I find a hope for me and all mankind. I would speak out in a world that is supposed to need no Savior beyond our human powers and say that the cross is for me the end of all self-sufficiency and the beginning of a life in harmony with the living God. I would speak out and say that here is the one who accepts us as we are, and who, as he makes us over in his likeness, never seeks to destroy that glorious difference that makes me me and you you — for he does not come to destroy but to fulfill.

And if "we cannot possibly give up speaking of the things that we have heard and seen," this also has to be clearly said: Christ awaits your decision. He is not an idea to be entertained amid a hundred others. He is a person who says: "Come unto me; and I will refresh you." He is a Lord who says, "Follow me."

13. *Moondust, Man and God*

> *When I consider thy heavens, the work of thy fingers, the moon and the stars which thou hast ordained; What is man, that thou art mindful of him? and the son of man, that thou visitest him?* PSALM 8:3-4

At 9:03 p.m. Pacific Standard Time on April 21, 1967, a robot arm jerked out and slowly descended onto the surface of the moon. Seven minutes later it came up with a scoop of dust a little over an inch in diameter. There it is still, that little machine some 240,000 miles up there, wiggling away in front of the television cameras, poised for another bite. Lots of things have happened since that April 21 — some of which I want to consider with you now — but somehow I can't forget this long-legged intruder pecking away at the surface of our moon. For this is the finger of man extended through the heavens for a pinch of moondust, like taking lunar snuff. Man the scientist has pushed past man the poet and said: "Now we'll show you, with absolute precision, whether or not it's made of green cheese." And has man the scientist not also elbowed aside man the worshipper, fingering the moondust and saying: "When I consider the heavens, the moon and the stars, this is what I find — and there is nothing anywhere, no angels and no god, that cannot be grabbed and analyzed like this?" Is that what he means, that little machine up there? He won't come back, you know. Man's finger never comes back once it has reached out to a new dimension of the universe. We're into a new era, whether we like it or not.

Some days after we had seen the little machine of

the future another picture filled our screens. We were in an ancient cathedral and the chanting of century-old psalms and prayers sounded in our ears. As we shared the mourning of the German people, Conrad Adenauer was laid to rest with the haunting and evocative liturgy of the Roman Catholic Church. Everyone said: "The end of an era." The great statesman was born in 1876, just after the Franco-Prussian war. He lived through the two World Wars to wrestle with the problems of the nuclear age. But, as he left us, surrounded by the panoply and symbols of the faith he deeply held, the page of history seemed to turn. Were the tolling bells of Cologne Cathedral ringing out the age of mystery, of man's fumbling and faltering, his obstinate reliance on an unseen God? And is that little machine up there on the moon tapping in the new age of clarity, of mastery, of man's reliance on his new and unsuspected powers?

This is the slick and simple conclusion that some would have us draw. The cathedral, and all it stands for, belongs to a shrouded past. The leaders of the future will have no need to seek guidance from the unseen, or inspiration from that which is beyond. The machine up there is signalling the great takeover. The heavens declare the glory of man, and the firmament showeth *his* handiwork. What more do we need? God vanishes before the probing light of human exploration, and man at last knows who he is, and what he can do. The liturgy of the new humanism is with us, and even some theologians are glad to join the chorus.

But is it all so simple? Is it really so obvious that God has disappeared, and that man is no longer a mystery? Granted that we are moving fast into a new age of unprecedented potential, and revolutionary outlook, are there any signs that man is any more master of his fate and arbiter of his destiny than when the psalms were written? Do we really think that mystery disappears as we analyze the moondust? And can anyone who has ever had a glimmering of real faith be talked out of his experience of God by any new logic of language or clatter of computers? I'm thrilled by that little machine pecking at the moon. I am also thrilled by the cathedral chorus of resurrection and eternal life. And I see no reason to think of one as the pointer to the future and the other as a quaint relic of the past. The little machine, in fact, could herald catastrophe as well as triumph; the cathedral can speak of the future with superb confidence and hope.

Let me remind you of something else that has happened since April 21. We have not only joined the German people in their tribute to a man of great age, full experience, and completed service. We have joined the Russian people in their great sorrow at the death of a young man, of great courage, brilliant potential, and service tragically incomplete. How does this tragedy fit into our thinking about the past and the future, about man and God? Surely here we have to pause and wonder again about the deeper questions that are as much a part of our space age as they were of any age before. I am not for a moment saying that this tragedy simply reminds us of the frailty and vulnerability of the human frame, still less that such a loss is some kind of warning against the pursuit of such new exploration. Every advance of the human spirit into the unknown has had its martyrs, but the quest goes on. This is rather what the death of the cosmonaut brings home to me: the ultimate mystery of man's questing spirit, and the astounding courage with which he greets the dangers of the unknown.

The triumphant breakthrough of modern technology, symbolized by that quivering machine that digs the moondust, is one thing. Another, and more important, is the strange compulsion behind the scientific effort, and the dedication of the men who volunteer to go visiting the moon. It is not, after all, that machine up there that is the miracle. It is, as always through the human story, the man — the first one who ventured into the sea, the first one who lit a fire, the Christopher Columbus, and the cosmonaut. There is no new age now upon us in which all these things are luminously clear, and man knows who he is and what he must do. The mystery of man — his restless desire to conquer his environment at endless cost to his safety and his comfort, his reaching after new horizons, physical, mental, and spiritual — remains. As the cosmonaut yields his young life the deep Why's of human nature are heard again, and we know that the answers will never be found in the textbooks of technology.

And so, within these same few days, we should not be surprised at another picture that has flashed upon our screens. Just when we have been assured that modern man not only has no need of God, but cannot even understand what such a concept means, we see the daughter of Joseph Stalin — the archpriest of an atheistic society — telling the world that "it is impossible to exist without God in my heart," and confessing that just five years ago she was baptized into the Christian church. We must respect her wishes not to exploit her testimony in the church, or anywhere else, but surely here is another sign that the simple dogma about the new era of the ticking machine taking over from the old era of cathedral bells is both shallow and false. We are still confronted with the age-old mysteries of both man and God.

"When I consider thy heavens, the work of thy fingers, the moon and the stars which thou hast ordained . . . ." Sure, we don't consider them exactly as the psalmist did. Into our consideration there presses a host of bewildering statistics, as we try to grasp the immensities of which the modern astronomer speaks. I can lie on a deckchair as a freighter slips through the darkness of the Atlantic on a summer night and gaze into the canopy of stars. I wonder what the author of this psalm would say if he were suddenly beside me and I explained what had been discovered about their distance and their motion. Once he had absorbed the thought that what we see is fabulously remote, and even so is but the edge of uncounted galaxies stretching away beyond all human powers of computing, I think he would say: "When I consider thy heavens, the work of thy fingers, the moon and the stars which thou hast ordained, what is man that thou art mindful of him?" And I would know what he meant. For surely the new picture of the universe rather adds to than diminishes the wonder of creation, and our sense of insignificance in the total picture. And belief in the being of God is completely unaffected. It is as easy to be an atheist when you think the moon is stuck up there perhaps ten miles away, as when you watch a man-made machine actually digging at its surface. If you believe, then the new universe that is disclosed simply adds to your sense of wonder; if you don't, it offers no confirmation of your disbelief.

Does anyone really think that the final mysteries will be disclosed as we analyze the moondust? And does the poetry vanish when we hold it in our hand? Is not our question, as we think of outer space, as we contemplate the energies that pulse within the smallest grain of dust, not the same as the psalmist's? "What is man?" Our first reaction to the immensities of the universe is exactly the same. What is man? What possible significance can this creature who clings for a few years to a minor planet, in a minor solar system, in one of an infinitude of galaxies, have in the total scheme of things? And if, like the psalmist, we believe in God, are we not even more likely to ask: "What is man that thou art mindful of him? and the son of man that thou visitest him?" Whether we believe in the God of the Christian creeds, or some great life force, or some impersonal creative power, how can we conceive that we, in this little corner, could be of any real concern to the Ultimate Spirit?

For the Christian the dilemma seems especially acute. For the more we give ourselves to thought of the vastness and wonder of creation, the less likely it seems that the Creator-God could concern himself with us. Our song of praise — "O Lord, our Lord, how excellent is thy name in all the earth! who hast set thy glory above the heavens" — seems almost to rule out the possibility of speaking to this Lord as children to a father. Yet as we follow this magnificent psalm right through we begin to see the answer. For at the very moment the psalmist has led us to the devastating question, "What is man that thou art mindful of him? or the son of man that thou visitest him?" he breaks into the most dazzling poem of man's uniqueness and glory ever penned.

"Thou hast made him a little lower than the angels, and hast crowned him with glory and honor. Thou hast made him to have dominion over the works of thy hands." With inspired insight we are shown the fantastic paradox of man's nature. On the one hand we are "babes and sucklings" who can only stammer the Creator's praise; on the other hand we are the destined lords of the universe, as the new translation says, "a little less than a god." Is this the wild guesswork of a Hebrew poet, or does it fit the factors of this complex world of today?

Well, what have we been thinking about as we reflected on recent pictures that have come to us from the world of today and tomorrow? We have a sense of wonder and bewilderment when we think of the moondust, that symbol of the infinitely small and infinitely huge, that reminder of our spatial insignificance and ultimate ignorance of the great beyond. We have been confronted with the enigma of death — whether it comes in the fullness of years or the bright promise of youth. We have been forced to realize how little we really know — about this world, or any other that may be attainable by man. We have felt the oppression of being swept along by a process we can neither fully understand nor control. In this mood the believer can only stammer his adoration like an infant, and the unbeliever confess his bewilderment and sometimes his despair.

But have we not also experienced a sense of exhilaration when we celebrated the human skills that sent that machine to collect the moondust? Have we not also given thanks for the warrior spirit of an Adenauer, the heroism of a cosmonaut? Have we not again recognized the spirit of freedom that no system, whether Communist or any other, can ever quench in the human heart? Is there not, in our present age, abundant evidence that man has a unique calling and destiny in this mysterious universe? And are there not signs that a generation reared to enjoy the benefits of technology is striking out again to the exploration of the eternal dimensions of love, beauty, true happiness — and God?

Too often it is supposed that the Christian attitude towards man's ambitions and achievements is to play them down with the reminder that we are merely creatures, and sinful creatures at that. It is indeed true that a spirit of worship and of reverence keeps us humble before God and a recognition of sin warns us of the dread possibility of catastrophe instead of triumph. But the Christian faith includes this vision of man "the viceroy of God," man to whom is given dominion over the world in which God has set him. "Thou hast put all things under his feet," is the warrant for our continual quest and restless exploration.

And I will show you something different from either
Your shadow at morning striding behind you
Or your shadow at evening arising to meet you:
I will show you fear in a handful of dust.

Yes: there is fear in the handful of moondust, fear of what man can do to himself in his pride and hate. But I will show you hope in a handful of dust, too, hope that man can pursue his quest for the fuller life that God has promised, hope that humility and love may guide the viceroys of God.

What is the ground for such hope? The author of the Epistle to the Hebrews addresses himself to that question. He quotes our psalm: "Thou hast put all things in subjection under him. For in that he put all things in subjection under him he left nothing (not even outer space) that is not put under him. But," he goes on, "we see not yet all things put under him." How right he is. Not only is there a vaster universe waiting for exploration than he ever dreamed, but man has not even got control over his own passions, his own demonic drives, his own selfishness and hates. "We see not yet all things put under him — but we see Jesus, who was made a little lower than the angels for the suffering of death, crowned with glory and honor."

What is he saying? "Not yet . . . but we see Jesus." This is the one enduring vision that accompanies the Christian, no matter what other images are flashing on his screen. We see Jesus. In him we see both the mystery of God revealed in terms we know, and words we can at least partly understand, and the mystery of man revealed as he truly is. When we see him we know that there is a Father who is mindful of us, that there is a God who has visited us. When we see him we know that there is hope for man to develop to new dimensions of self-mastery and love. For it is in Jesus that the Creator-God has come near to us at the very deepest point of our need and despair, and to know him is to be lifted with him towards the true glory that God has designed for his human family.

This is what we seek when we meet together here for worship — to bring all the pictures that have flashed on the screens of our minds and hearts so that in them and through them we may see Jesus the Christ, who holds the secret of both God and man.

14. *The God of Luck*

> *But if not, then we shall know that it is not his hand that smote us; it was a chance that happened to us.* I SAMUEL 6:9

Chance, luck, fortune — we don't use these words much in church. They don't seem to belong. In our common prayers we appeal to a sovereign God in whose love and grace we try to confide and not to the pagan goddess of Fortune. We are not likely to abandon singing "Guide me, O thou great Jehovah," in exchange for "With a little bit of luck." Yet I'm sure there is no one reading this now who has never wondered about the element of chance in human affairs and in his own life. We admit that it's there by the things we say: "Good luck," we say to a friend setting off for a day's fishing, since we know very well that it won't be just his skill that will bring home the catch. "What a happy chance," we say, "that the fire on the *Hanseatic* broke out when she was in dock," and I might well have said, if she had chanced to be at sea, that I was extremely lucky, since I had originally booked a passage on her for that voyage. We talk about the luck of the draw, the chance of the draft, the fortunes of war. And behind this common talk about luck there must lie this serious question, for a Christian as for anybody else: "How big a part does sheer chance play? Or is there behind even the most random event some kind of hidden direction and meaning?"

The Old Testament story we read this morning shows us an ancient people wrestling with this same problem, and the rather curious method they adopted to solve it. The Philistines in the course of their constant warring with the Israelites had come into possession of Israel's most sacred symbol — the ark of the covenant. During the period when they kept the ark in the temple of Dagon a plague struck and the Philistines suffered an epidemic of what the King James Version call "emerods." Scholars tell us that this was really boils caused by bubonic plague. In those days the popular response was not to look for the source of infection and take prophylactic measures but to seek to placate some deity who may have been offended. It naturally occurred to some that the whole thing was the result of having the ark, this holy symbol of their enemy's god, in their midst. Yet even in those days there was no certainty that this plague had such a definite cause. It might just be a matter of luck. So they thought up a simple way to decide the matter.

The ark of the Israelites was solemnly placed on a cart and surrounded by golden ornaments representing the plague that had afflicted them. A couple of cows were hitched to the cart and they were led to the frontier not far from Beth-shemesh, the nearest Israelite town. As their calves were left behind, the chances were that they would turn back to find them. But if they went ahead in the direction of Beth-shemesh it would be taken as a sign that it was indeed the God of Israel who had brought the plague upon the land. What the Philistines were doing was really to try to solve the problem of luck by appealing to chance yet again — which just shows you how difficult this whole business is! Off went the cart and the die was cast: "See, if it goeth up by the way of his own coast to Beth-shemesh then he hath done us this great evil: but if not, then we shall know that it was not his hand that smote us; it was a chance that happened to us."

It is a vivid picture that is painted for us and there was no doubt about the result. "The kine took the straight way to the way of Beth-shemesh, and went along the highway, lowing as they went, and turned not aside to the right hand or to the left; and the lords of the Philistines went after them unto the border . . . ." The instinct of the cows had settled the matter for the Philistines.

It was indeed the God of Israel who had been afflicting them — and not sheer chance.

Translate that story into modern terms and you have exactly the dilemma that still haunts us. God or chance? The God of the Bible or the God of luck? Or are our lives determined by some queer mixture of both? We don't avoid the problem by saying that for us today there is another explanation. It's no solution to say that this epidemic was neither the direct action of God, nor sheer chance, but the result of germs breeding in unsanitary surroundings. For there still remains the agonizing question of why any particular person should be the victim of the germ, why one tribe and not another. We know infinitely more today about the causes of disease but are still baffled by the element of chance in its incidence. Even if we knew exactly why one person is vulnerable to a germ and another immune we still have to ask: "Is there any rhyme or reason why they should have been made this way. And isn't it just chance that leads us into an area of infection? Or just luck that healing is available for one who lives in this place, and not for the other unfortunate who lives somewhere else?"

I believe that most of us who have some kind of religious belief today have worked out a kind of practical philosophy whereby we acknowledge that there is an area of chance in all human activities and experience but believe that we can, beyond and within this area, distinguish the guidance and direction of God. This or that may happen, we say, according to random chance, but ultimately we are in the hands of God. Or we may like to distinguish between the part of our life where things just seem to happen fortuitously and that part where we are conscious of God's direction. Few of us have worked out a very coherent philosophy, but the average modern Christian seems to rub along on some sort of compromise like this. And many of us suspect that the state of our religious health — or, if you like, the strength of our faith — can generally be measured by the expanding or contracting of these two segments of life. The closer we are to God the more the area of sheer chance seems to shrink; the weaker our faith the more we leave to luck.

In the light of the Bible, as well as our daily experience, we have to accept a considerable amount of what looks like sheer chance. "I saw," says the writer of Ecclesiastes, "that the race is not to the swift, nor the battle to the strong, neither yet bread to the wise, nor yet riches to men of understanding, nor yet favor to men of skill: but time and chance happeneth to them all." This most sophisticated of Bible writers had come to the conclusion that the rewards we get in this life are by no means always predictable according to our virtues — "time" and "chance" intervene and upset all our calculations.

The New Testament has no such philosophic comment to offer on this question, but the element of chance is assumed in the encounters of men with Christ and their freedom of choice when confronted with his demands. "By chance," we read in the parable of the Good Samaritan, "there came down a certain priest that way." We are often left wondering at the element of chance in the whole story of the arrest and trial of the Lord. If he had not gone to Jerusalem at that time . . . ? If Judas had decided not to betray him . . . ? If Pilate had followed his own inclination instead of the demand of the crowd . . . ? And what about the appeal to chance which we see in the action of the apostles later when they wanted to fill the vacant place left by the defection of Judas? It is something of a shock for the modern Christian to realize that one of the apostles was chosen in a lottery.

Yet the moment we raise these questions we find that they are countered by a quite different emphasis that is typical of the Bible. Time and again we are told that what looked like sheer accident was indeed part of a mysterious plan of God. Peter had been through the terrible chances and accidents that led to the crucifixion, yet in his first speech at Pentecost he speaks of Jesus "being delivered by the determinate counsel and foreknowledge of God." The epistles show us clearly that for all the apostles the crucifixion was no accident. Human wickedness and free choice had indeed converged to produce this fearful crime, but chance alone was not left to triumph in the darkness of Calvary. "Though he was crucified through weakness, yet he liveth by the power of God."

The really astonishing thing about the Bible is how

seldom in fact any word of "chance," "luck" or "fortune" occurs. The Bible is concerned with the kingdom of God, and in that kingdom there is no accident or luck. And as that kingdom presses in upon our human life, as men and women come to enter it and live in it here and now, so the element of chance recedes and the hand of God appears. The area of chance is seen to be real, and often baffling, but the Bible writers are convinced that it is surrounded by the ocean of God's kingdom, his holy will and love. Therefore, no matter how chance may reign, the ultimate control is always his. This is what our forefathers meant when they talked of the sovereignty of God. They were not fatalists, but neither did they see themselves as helpless victims of fortune, of good or bad. In times of adversity, instead of cursing their luck, they held on, sustained by the conviction that God's kingdom is invincible. For they remembered that night when sheer evil fortune seemed to conspire to deliver their Lord to his enemies, and they were nourished by his supreme assurance of the Father's presence and his contagious prayer: "nevertheless not what I will, but what thou wilt."

When we live in the kingdom there is no such thing as sheer luck. Our business as Christians is steadily to expand our experience of that kingdom so that, more and more, in this world of uncertainty and insecurity, we can distinguish the guidance of God. It may be that this is going to be the true distinguishing mark of religious faith in the days ahead of us. For just as we may steadily grow into the kingdom where we see all things in the light of God's holy will, and seek to bring our wills in line with his; so we may go the other way. When faith fails, then more and more of our experience begins to look like sheer chance. When we cease to have an active belief in a guiding and controlling God, then with a slow but inevitable mutation we shall begin to worship the God of luck.

It is already beginning to happen. When we ponder on the picture of the origin of the known universe as science discloses it to us, the strange chances, for instance, that led to the emergence of this solar system, the odds against this earth's appearing with temperature and vegetation to sustain life, the extraordinary coincidence of conditions that led to man's appearance, and the prodigality of nature by which one in a billion cells may live; when we think about our own conception and the hazard of our birth; when we think of the dancing of the chromosomes and the juggling of the genes that produced you and me — and not someone else — then we have to make a kind of basic decision. Either all this is sheer luck, what Bertrand Russell called the "fortuitous concourse of atoms"; or it is mechanically determined, the operation of blind fate; or it is a fraction of the plan and purpose of a mighty God whom we cannot hope entirely to comprehend but whom we can trust, because in our darkness he has shined enough light for us to find his will and do it.

Blind fate is the answer of those philosophies that find in history the working of some ineluctable law, like that of Dialectical Materialism. But far more popular in the western world today is the worship of the God of luck. It is as if many have come to say: "So it was sheer chance that produced the universe; sheer chance that brought me here at this hour; sheer chance that will determine when my life snuffs out. Life is a gamble — so what the hell?" This may account for the gambling passion that is sweeping our western world. Games of chance for fun is one thing — human beings have always been fascinated by the toss of dice, the fortune of the cards, the spin of a coin. But gambling as a fever, a compulsion, is quite another. It reflects an inner abandonment of hope for real purpose and meaning, either for ourselves or for our world.

Hence the supreme importance of what we are doing now. Here we are with all kinds of different experiences of what is called good and bad fortune, and all kinds of different interpretations. But here we seek to worship not the God of luck, but the God and Father of our Lord Jesus Christ. We steady ourselves on the ultimate conviction that this is the heart of all things, the love of God as it is revealed to us in the life, death and resurrection of our Lord. Can anyone face the cross of Christ and mutter: "What bad luck?" Can anyone receive the bread and wine as symbols of a purely fortuitous calamity long ago? No: here we know that through all the mystery of evil and of suffering, through all the chances and changes of our mortal life, we may follow the path of the kingdom where God's will is done, and live by the prayer "as in heaven so on earth — beginning in me."

15. *No Chameleon Christians*

And be not conformed to this world; but be ye transformed by the renewing of your mind, that ye may prove what is that good, and acceptable, and perfect will of God.
ROMANS 12:2

"Be ye not conformed to this world: but be ye transformed by the renewing of your mind." The New English Bible reads: "Adapt yourselves no longer to the pattern of this present world, but let your minds be remade and your whole nature thus transformed." The translation of J. B. Phillips goes like this: "Don't let the world around you squeeze you into its own mold, but let God remold your minds from within."

One way or another we can hardly miss the meaning. The immediate target of the apostle's admonition was a group of Christians trying to live by the gospel in the precarious environment of imperial Rome, but it surely comes with equal power and urgency to the conscience of church members in metropolitan New York. The squeeze of the world around us is just as powerful, and much more subtle, than it was for them. This is an awkward Word of God to us, an uncomfortable Word, for it runs counter to our instincts in an urban church, and to the prevailing philosophy of our day. We've not been raised to be different; the pressure on us has steadily been to conform, to adapt, to fit smoothly into the society around us. According to a popular theory of education, the real point of schooling is not so much to acquire knowledge or character as to be compatible, to be easily assimilated into what is called our "peer group." Then we are exposed to the mass media — radio and television, the magazines and newspapers, the movies and advertising — which, with all their diversity, tend to promote a common point of view and pattern of behavior. We easily become the victims of clichés and slogans rather than individuals with opinions and standards of our own. A sign of this is the gradual disappearance of the "character," the eccentric who left his mark on the community, the university, or political life. In public life today the magic word is consensus. Politicians, leaders of industry and labor — yes, and we ministers too — love to feel that we have the mass of opinion on our side. The temptation is not to form an opinion and then seek to sway the masses, but to poll the masses and then announce that this is our opinion. We don't want to be the odd man out. The squeeze is on, and by and large we are anxious to conform.

This may not be quite so true today as a decade ago. For this is a period of protest as well as conformity. In reaction to the climate of the consensus the younger generation in particular is erupting in an orgy of defiance, eccentricity, and revolt. Yet this very easily produces a new kind of conformity. When we are told not to conform to "this world," this world may be for us the conventional world of the Establishment. But our world might equally well be that of academic radicalism, or of the coffee bar and discotheque. Among the bearded beatniks the nonconformist is the man in the grey flannel suit. (I never felt more out of fashion than when I strolled through Carnaby Street in London this summer!) The point of our text is not that the Christian must always be in revolt against the established order, but that he must resist the temptation to adjust his convictions to the crowd around him and to let himself be squeezed into whatever the fashionable mold may be. We may admire the ability of the chameleon in self-defense to take on the color and pattern of his environment but there is nothing admirable in the Christian who is a mere reflection of the world he lives in. *No chameleon Christians!* is the Word of God for us.

But this is not the whole Word. It must have occurred to you already that "Be not conformed to this world" could be a very sterile and negative philosophy. For some people, indeed, it is a lot easier to be the odd man out than the even man in. They revel in being different, in being difficult, in casting the one negative vote. Others find satisfaction in being out of fashion. They stick to old opinions, like old clothes, and delight in defying whatever the current vogue may be. We sometimes give young people the impression that being a Christian means disapproving of everything that is up-to-date, and continually saying, like the winetaster in the Bible, "The old is better." The church often seems to be saying: "It's new; therefore it's dangerous; don't go along." A closer look at our text will show that St. Paul meant nothing of this kind. There's not a line in the New Testament to suggest that the Christian must resist the world around him simply by sticking to the patterns of the past, and refusing to move with the times. If the chameleon is not our model, neither is the dinosaur. Nobody has better obeyed the injunction "Be not conformed" than the prehistoric animals, and nobody is more extinct. No dinosaur Christians!

"Be not conformed to this world: *but be ye transformed by the renewing of your mind.*" There is nothing negative in the nonconformity of the Christian. We are being told that we need not be at the mercy of the world around us, need not be subject to the pressures of popular opinion, need not be afraid to be different, for we have access to a transforming power, the springs of renewal for the human spirit. The greatest achievements in history have not been the work of men who were entirely in tune with the spirit of their age; nor of men who were stubbornly rooted in the past. Abraham Lincoln and Winston Churchill were able to resist at the right moment the climate of their times, not through sheer conservatism, but because of a deeper insight that transformed them and renewed their minds. So in religion every revitalizing movement has come from those, like the prophets of Israel or the apostles of Christ, who refused to go along with the contemporary current of opinion, not because they were enslaved by old ideas but because they had a vision of something new. The true symbol of the Christian is neither the chameleon nor the dinosaur, but the mythical phoenix — the bird that periodically submitted to be burned and rose again in glory from the ashes. There are times when the Christian, when the church, must die to the powers of this world in order to rise again with resurrection power of Christ. The Christian word is neither conformity nor nonconformity, but transformation — transformation by the renewing of the mind.

We need to hear this again right now. For in every section of the church today a debate is raging between those who in the name of "aggiornamento" want to adjust Christian beliefs and Christian practice to the spirit of the age, and those who want at all costs to cling to the creeds and customs of the past. The one side cries: "Get with it: accept the new world we live in. Adapt your doctrines to the modern mind and swing with the tempo of today." The other shouts: "Back to the Bible: stand by the old creeds. The old-time religion is good enough for me." In the light of our text surely both are wrong. The way forward is neither a capitulation to the spirit of the age — "be not conformed to this world" — nor obstinate clinging to the status quo — "be ye transformed by the renewing of your minds." The words "liberal" and "conservative" have really no business in the church. The word is truth, transforming and renewing truth, whatever it costs and wherever it may lead. The voice we need to listen to, above the clatter of our controversy, is that which says: "I am the way, the truth, and the life." The Christian church is neither the slave of current fashion, nor shackled to its past. It must stand above all else for the transforming power of Christ.

The church's purpose must be to bring men and women into the transforming presence of Christ. This seems to me the note that is often missing in the debates, the controversies, the experiments, and the pronouncements of the church today. There are serious questions to be discussed about new theology, new confessions, social action, changes in worship, the ecumenical movement. But basic to them all is the vital question: Does the Christian church stand for something quite unique? Does it offer a gospel that can really renew our minds and transform our lives? It is that we should pause to think about — whether we are temperamentally on the side of change or of the status quo. So much of our thinking is on the level of how the church can compete in the modern world. Among the many voices that sound about us, have we not ears to hear the one that says: "Not as the world giveth, give I unto you." "Not as the world . . ." — there is a unique transforming power in the gospel of Christ, and it is this above all that we are committed to find, to experience, and to proclaim.

Recently I have tried to absorb some of the books that are offering new and radically disturbing versions of the Christian message. Insofar as any book that is thoughtful and honest stimulates a renewing of the mind I am grateful for it. But what astonishes me about most of them is the assumption that the Christian gospel must be made completely compatible with current fashions of thought — secularism, scientific humanism, analytic philosophy, or whatever it may be. Time and again we are told that this or that Christian doctrine is no longer acceptable to what is called the "modern mind," and therefore must be restated or discarded. No hint is given that perhaps, after all, the Christian gospel contains some unique truth, some transforming power that cannot be entirely squared with any current philosophy — in this or any other age. The words: "Be not conformed *to this world*" literally mean "to this age"; in other words, to the prevailing climate of thought. When we are told that since this is an age of secularism, then the gospel must be interpreted in purely secular terms, what is this but sheer conformity to this age? Surely the task of the Christian at such a time is neither to capitulate to the prevailing fashion of thought, nor just to damn it in the name of old-time religion, but to face it in joyful confession of him who can transform us all by the renewing of our minds.

We live in times of violent and revolutionary change. Agreed. And in such times the Christian revolution in our hearts and minds is more relevant than ever. Some knowledge of how in the past the gospel has been a force of change and renewal should help us to withstand the defeatism that bows to the prevailing wind. We are summoned to "discern the signs of the times" — to be aware of the mighty forces that are blowing through our world — but we are not required to submit to any doctrine of inevitability. Too often as Christians today we seem to share the fatalism that talks in terms of irresistible forces, of "winds of change," of "waves of the future" — as if the trends of this world are irreversible and unstoppable. When I hear such talk I remember a day when a young soldier of Rommel's panzer army, riding in triumph through the roads of northern France in the summer of 1940, spotted in the endless column of prisoners going the other way a young chaplain in his faded clerical collar. He leaped from this tank and said to me something like this: "The day of the church is over. It's a new world now — and nothing can stop us." Why should we accept in any age the philosophy of inevitability that the world offers us? "Not as the world giveth, give I unto you." We have another philosophy, that of the sovereign God and the Savior Christ, to transform our outlook and renew our minds.

There is another area where today we are being urgently asked to conform to this world. Everyone knows that there is what is called a "moral revolution" going on. Whether we read about it in magazines, or experience it in our own families and businesses, none of us can escape the restlessness and questioning about the ethical standards of our day. Nearly always when this is discussed it is the morals of sex and marriage that are in question. For some older people this is a confusing and disturbing area of which they are often just the puzzled spectators. But for the younger generation of Christians this is an urgent, and often agonizing practical question. Many find themselves in an environment where traditional restraints have been abandoned, where any ideal of chastity is ridiculed, where a cynical view is taken of all marriage vows. And the pressure is strong to be "conformed to this world." "Go along; don't be awkward; there are no rules any more." It is surely not enough for the church simply to reiterate old negative commandments, or merely to condemn what is called "laxity and promiscuity." We need to stress again the positive values that lie behind the discipline of the Christian ethic. We need to demonstrate the transforming power of Christ in this area too. And we need to proclaim the spiritual power that lies in a renewing of the mind. The word of Christ may seem stern, but it comes from one who knows us through and through, who came not to destroy any good human instinct but to fulfill. The fashion of the world may well offer temporary satisfactions at the cost of real fulfillment. "Not as the world giveth, give I unto you."

Don't let the world squeeze you into its own mold, but let God remold your minds from within. We are here because we believe that this is possible. There is nothing dramatic or sensational about the process of remolding. Indeed, there have been people whose minds seem to have been turned inside out in one encounter with the living Christ. St. Paul himself had an experience like this on the Damascus Road. But the New Testament confirms the experience of most of us that this is a slow business, with many setbacks. The important thing is to know that it can happen, and go on happening at whatever stage in life we are. In our private prayers, in our public worship, in listening to the Word, in receiving the sacrament, in the experience of Christian friendship, in the attempt to obey the voice of the Spirit in our daily life, in our concern for justice, in our practice of mercy — in all these and many others God can be remolding our minds from within. If it is truly happening we shall be less and less at the mercy of current opinion and the pressures of our day. We shall find truer standards for judgment, grow more charitable in our responses to others, shed some of our prejudices and foolish habits of thought. Thus, says the apostle, "you will prove that the plan of God for you is good." And isn't that exactly what we are often inclined to doubt?

No chameleon Christians! No dinosaur Christians! Not conformed, but transformed. Not adapted but remade, rising like a phoenix from the ashes of our past. Not squeezed into the world's mold, but remolded from within. That should be our program and our purpose.

16. *What Joyful Noise?*

> *Make a joyful noise unto the Lord, all ye lands. Serve the Lord with gladness: come before his presence with singing.*
>
> PSALM 100:1-2

Since I often draw your attention to alternative translations of a Bible text, let me begin by offering you a revised substandard version of Psalm 100:

> Make a dismal noise unto the Lord, all ye lands. Serve the Lord with sadness: come before his presence with groaning. Know ye that the Lord he is a dead image: it is we that have made him, and not he himself.

If there is one thing that can be said without qualification about the skeptical, cynical, self-flagellating mood that has infected the church today it is that it has smothered the joyful noise. The killjoys used to be the Puritans — those who, as Macaulay said, objected to bear-baiting not because it gave pain to the bear but because it gave pleasure to the spectators. Some of us have known this kind of Puritanism, where worship was dreary, sermons a long lament, prayers an interminable moan, and laughter regarded as a desecration of the Sabbath. There are still some places where a repressive and self-righteous orthodoxy casts a shadow of gloom and disapproval over all that is joyful and exuberant. But in the church as we know it heresy, not orthodoxy, is the killjoy. By heresy I mean the denials and negations that abound in much current paperback theology, the rejection of Christian truths in which millions have rejoiced, the assimilation of the faith to the trend of the secular world. Whatever else may be said for the exponents of radical theology and the eloquent morticians of the church, they cannot be said to have liberated a new spring of gaiety and joy. Even those most concerned for renewal and reform seem to be bogged down in the solemn jargon of endless self-studies and reports.

When we used to talk about building bridges between the church and the secular world the hope was that the traffic would be lit by the hope and gaiety of the gospel. The church needed to receive all that was true, honest, and lovely in the secular world; and the world to be challenged by a Word of hope and joy. Instead it seems that across these bridges there has poured into the church a torrent of cynicism, angst, peevishness, and gloom. This is not the whole truth, but I have a feeling that one of the apostles visiting our churches today, attending our courts and conferences, might say: "You are a serious people; you are a worried people; you are a busy people — but where in all this welter of worship and activity, in all this deliberation and debate, where is the joyful noise?"

I know the answer that we are all ready to give. "What," we say, "is there to be joyful about? Can we feel like breaking out into singing in a world like this, where two-thirds of the population are hungry and there are 60,000,000 more mouths to feed every year, where there is a terrible war going on in Vietnam, where children are mobbed and beaten because of the color of their skins, where vicious criminals break into happy homes to maim and to slaughter, where thousands are seeking escape in drugs, and everyone lives under the shadow of the bomb."

I know also how easily a chirpy religion of hollow optimism will offend the sensitive, and insult the intelligence of our contemporaries. There is a kind of "joyful noise" which sounds ominously like the warbling of Nero's fiddle. Some suspect that we come to church simply to escape from the worries of modern life, to huddle together for our heavenly music while the world goes to hell. No one really wants a "joyful noise" that is little more than a temporary and self-centered forgetfulness, an empty-headed whistling in the dark. Anyone who has been through the dark waters knows how futile are the consolations of the merely cheerful. There are times when the last thing you want is this kind of "joyful noise."

But what is this book from which we hear the summons to "make a joyful noise unto the Lord"? Is it an omnibus volume of assorted optimism, a collection of happy thoughts to distract our minds, and enable us to forget the sorrows of the world? The book of Psalms alone is sufficient to dispel any such idea. "Out of the depths have I cried unto thee, O Lord." "O God, why hast thou cast us off for ever?" "From the end of the earth will I cry unto thee, when my heart is overwhelmed." "My heart is sore pained within me; and the terrors of death are fallen upon me." "Behold, thou desirest truth in the inward parts." "Why art thou cast down, O my soul? and why art thou disquieted within me?" "All thy waves and thy billows have gone over me." "My God, my God, why hast thou forsaken me?" Are these the words of men whose religion is bright and easy? The Word of God comes to us through the psalms as a Word that pierces to the depths. There is nothing here to suggest that faith and hope and joy are reached along a sunlit road that bypasses the valley of the shadow.

And so it is throughout the Bible. The problems and agonies that we list in protest against the "joyful noise" are to be found in abundance in its pages. It reflects every horror and misery that man can know, and the song that breaks through is no surface melody, but rises from the depths. Scholars tell us that Psalm 100 was written after the Exile, when the survivors struggled back to Jerusalem and rebuilt the ruined Temple. Think what that means. A tiny people, whose country had been plundered and ruined, whose hopes had been shattered, whose fathers had been hauled into captivity, who were surrounded by mighty empires that ignored or despised their God, had the audacity to stand up and sing: "Make a joyful noise unto the Lord, all ye lands. Serve the Lord with gladness: come before his presence with singing." To the listening world this might be crazy, this might be absurd, but it was not the lighthearted effervescence of those who "had never had it so good."

So it is in the New Testament. I can think of two occasions when we hear of a song, the "joyful noise" of praise.

One is the time when a group of men met in the darkness to have their last meal with their Lord. As the powers of evil that we know today — hatred, jealousy, treachery, mob violence, brutality, and fear — closed around the Son of God, the solemn words were spoken of acceptance and of sacrifice: "This is my body . . . broken for you." "This is my blood . . . shed for many." Then, we are told, "when they had sung an hymn, they went out into the mount of Olives." A joyful noise at this dreadful moment? Yes: for this is the moment when we hear the words: "Ye shall be sorrowful, but your sorrow shall be turned into joy. A woman when she is in travail hath sorrow, because her hour is come: but as soon as she is delivered of the child, she remembereth no more the anguish, for joy that a man is born into the world. And ye now therefore have sorrow: but I will see you again, and your heart shall rejoice, and your joy no man taketh from you."

Soon they were to know exactly what that meant. For the other incident that comes to mind is that of Paul and Silas, when they had been arrested, flogged, and fastened to the stocks in jail. That was their reward for trying to serve their Lord and spread his gospel of love. How would you feel, isolated in prison, with your body aching in every joint, and your future a horrible question mark? This is how *they* felt: "At midnight Paul and Silas prayed, and sang praises unto God: and the prisoners heard them."

I choose these examples to show that the "joyful noise" we are considering is not the hollow gaiety of an escapist cult, or an untried faith. But, of course, the "joyful noise" is not always wrung from moments of trial and danger. The fact we have so often forgotten these days is that the Bible speaks of joy at the very heart of creation, in the life of God himself. It is there in the beginning "when the morning stars sang together, and all the sons of God shouted for joy." It is there in the end when "the ransomed of the Lord shall return, and come to Zion with songs and everlasting joy upon their heads: they shall obtain joy and gladness, and sorrow and sighing shall flee away." Even the fiercest books of the Bible have at least some echo of the "joyful noise" and in the center comes the announcement of the gospel: "Behold, I bring you good tidings of great joy, which shall be to all people."

Do we really believe that God is ultimately not only holy, not only infinite, not only love — but also joy? So long as we are debating whether God can be conceived in any personal way at all, so long as we are obsessed with our own attempts to figure out the mystery, so long as we are crushed by the problems of humanity, so long as we are seeking a purely secular solution to all our dilemmas, God will be for us neither love nor joy. And no "joyful noise" can rise from a soul that struggles with abstractions, or a church that has lost the vision of the eternal. Some years ago Baron Von Hugel, the Roman Catholic layman who enriched the thought and devotion of Christians of all persuasions, fought against the subjectivism that seems to leave God at the mercy of our human experience. He even resisted the idea, so fashionable today, that God is in some way the suffering victim of the powers of evil. For him, with his delicacy of spirit and profound experience of pain and sorrow, God was ultimately joy. This was for him the liberating center of faith. "We will thus rest content," he wrote, "with an outlook, obscure and fragmentary in parts, but with the tracts of glorious richness, variety, drama and tension, the whole lit up, sustained and vitalized by a continually renewed conviction of the Perfect Goodness, the Pure Joy of God" (*Essays and Addresses,* 11, 210).

We are so accustomed to being confronted with demands, with problems, with theological puzzles, with analyses of the world around us, in our worship today that it is not surprising that the note of sheer adoration, of joy in the being and presence of our God, has almost died away. What should be the explosive point of communal praise — the singing of our hymns — has tended to become a kind of option in which some participate and others don't. And many of the hymns in our book are infected by the subjectivism and introspection that is the death-knell of true praise. There is room for the occasional song of meditation and pious hope, but look at the space they occupy compared with the sections devoted to sheer adoration and joy in God.

I believe it would be for the health of the church, and

for the good of our souls, if we had a new explosion of "joyful noise unto the Lord." We need new hymns of pure celebration of God in the language of our day. We need new music of joyful adoration. Meanwhile there are riches to be used and voices to contribute. We are immensely grateful that we have in this church a lively and dedicated ministry of music. They know that their task is not to perform to an audience but to voice both *for* and *with* the congregation our common adoration of God and celebration of his works. They are, if I may put it that way, the captains of the joyful noise in this house of God.

They stand in a great tradition. It is characteristic of the religion of the Bible that God should be praised in song. The psalms of Israel were chanted by both choirs and people. This hundredth psalm would be sung responsively as the people assembled for worship. The congregation approaching the Temple door would raise a mighty voice: "Make a joyful noise unto the Lord, all ye lands," while from within would come the answering melody of the Temple choirs: "Serve the Lord with gladness: come before his presence with singing."

There is nothing peripheral about the ministry of music in the Christian church. The earliest scrap of information we have from outside sources about the earliest Christian worship is a letter from a Roman Governor to the Emperor, describing what the Christians were up to in his province. "They meet in the early morning," he wrote, "and sing a hymn to Christ as God." The gospel spread over the ancient world, not as a subject for debate, and not as an interesting philosophy, but as a "joyful noise." The inherent joy of the Christian message overflowed in song. So it has been in every renewal and reformation of the church. St. Francis sang:

All creatures of our God and King,
Lift up your voice with us and sing.

and summoned the whole family of man and nature to an outburst of praise. The Reformation released a mighty volume of song to celebrate the rediscovered glory and grace of God. "Now thank we all our God," they sang across Europe, and "A mighty fortress is our God." The

Calvinist psalm-tunes were such a surprising and popular outburst of praise that Queen Elizabeth referred to them as "these Geneva jigs." (Not the usual picture of Calvinism!) When John Wesley roused the church in eighteenth-century England, his brother Charles was beside him to provide for the "joyful noise" that swept the country with no less than 6,500 hymns.

Wherever faith in God is lit, or relit, wherever the gospel becomes a real power in men's lives, there will be song. It may be the resurrection glory of a Hallelujah Chorus; or it may be the poignant moment when we are lifted through anguish to that strange joy that the world can neither give nor take away — suggested by the haunting lines of Siegfried Sassoon written in the trenches of World War I:

Everyone suddenly burst out singing:
And I was filled with such delight
As prisoned birds must find in freedom
Winging wildly across the white
Orchards and dark green fields: on; on;
and out of sight.
Everyone's voice was suddenly lifted
And beauty came like the setting sun.
My heart was shaken with tears: and horror
Drifted away . . . O but everyone
Was a bird; and the song was wordless.
The singing will never be done.

"Make a joyful noise unto the Lord, all ye lands . . ." — this is not just the cozy singing of a special group of people, keeping up their spirits. It is an invitation to the world around us. They were bold men and women who summoned the great pagan empires to rejoice with them in their God. Are we bold enough today to summon our pagan world to the celebration of the Lord who made us and redeemed us? Anyone drifting into a church like this today can sense the reality and power of the Christian gospel through the singing of our hymns quite as much as by what is said from the pulpit. Thus we believe: thus we pray — and thus we *sing*. The world is waiting for that "joyful noise."

•

17. *Loyalty-Test for Christians*

> *So when they had dined, Jesus saith to Simon Peter, Simon, son of Jonas, lovest thou me more than these? He saith unto him, Yea, Lord; thou knowest that I love thee. He saith unto him, Feed my lambs.* JOHN 21:15

The word "loyalty-test" raises mixed emotions with us today. On the one hand we recognize that a government, a party, a club — and even a church — has the right to ask some sort of pledge of allegiance and to exert at least some form of discipline to insure loyalty to such a pledge. (If I were a member of the Flat Earth Society I should expect to be asked to declare my belief that the earth is flat, and to be censured or expelled if I was discovered saying that it was round, or oval, or anything else.) On the other hand we find it distasteful to pry into the lives of our neighbors with a view to discovering how loyal they may be, and we are doubtful whether really fair and adequate tests can ever be devised.

Let me assure you right away that I am not going to talk in this sermon about loyalty-tests for Christians as a means of probing into the lives, the opinions, the convictions of fellow members of the church. In this context there is one test that matters. It is the test we apply to ourselves in the presence of God. A few verses after the passage that we are going to explore here we find Peter pointing to another disciple and saying, "Lord, and what shall this man do?" and the answer he gets is brusque: "What is that to thee? Follow thou me." I am speaking to those who have heard this command

"Follow thou me" and are concerned to test their own, and not someone else's, loyalty to Christ.

The majority of us have at some time or other publicly confessed our belief in Jesus Christ as Savior and Lord, and have promised to be his faithful disciple. I am sure that, like me, you ask yourself from time to time: "Just what kind of a Christian am I? How much does my membership in Christ's church really mean to me? If it came to the test how strong would my loyalty actually be?" These are healthy questions to ask from time to time. To be always asking them, always tormenting oneself about one's faith, always rooting about our souls with a kind of morbid introspection is, of course, unhealthy, but I believe that God has provided for us certain times when we ought to say: "Well, how about it? How Christian am I?" Never mind about old so-and-so who seems so much better a Christian than I am, or about that other one who doesn't seem to measure up — what's that to thee? There are moments, and Holy Communion is certainly one of them, when each of us is in the real presence of Christ. He puts the loyalty-question: each of us answers for himself.

This story of Peter's dialogue with the risen Lord is the ending of the Fourth Gospel. It's as if this book, which is totally unlike any other ever written, had something climactic to say. The figure of Christ who moves through these pages with such a warm humanity and such a haunting divinity leaves us with a simple question. The recorded words that have ranged the heights and depths of the human spirit, stretching the understanding of the most devout and brilliant minds in every Christian age, are now concentrated in one very simple question: "Lovest thou me?" Perhaps if we divest this text of its antique clothing and listen to what was heard by the original listeners to this Gospel we may recapture its startling simplicity: "After breakfast, Jesus said to Simon Peter, 'Simon, son of John, do you love me more than all else?' "

"Do you love me?" How many times has that question been asked by men and women? And how astonishing that the story of the Son of God, set out for us in this Gospel as a cosmic battle of light with darkness, life with death, love with hate, should end with such a homely —

some would say a sentimental — query. If this had been the record of an ordinary man, even the best who ever lived, there would be something banal, or even embarrassing about this scene. But it is Jesus Christ, God incarnate, the Lord who rose from the dead, who speaks like this, and the "love" of which he speaks has overtones that drown out any merely romantic associations in our minds. I'm not going to plunge into any elaborate distinctions in the Greek words for love and tell you that this is a love of totally different quality and meaning from all you normally mean by human affection. The writer in fact uses two different words in this one passage, and I don't believe he wanted us to worry about distinguishing them. The word certainly carries with it part of what anyone means when he asks, "Do you love me?" (It's a thin religion that rules out the emotions and affections of the human heart.) But when this Jesus Christ puts such a question to us it is the total loyalty and direction of our lives that is at stake. Behind it throbs the great commandment: "Thou shalt love the Lord thy God with all thy heart, and with all thy soul, and with all thy strength, and with all thy mind; and thy neighbor as thyself."

We don't care too much today for what you might call "love-talk" about Christ. The sugary language of devotion that has been used in the church rings false in many ears. We sing the hymns of our forefathers: "How sweet the name of Jesus sounds in a believer's ear"; "More love to thee, O Christ, more love to thee!", but few of us would write that way today. When I hear a modern congregation singing, "Be my last thought, how sweet to rest for ever on my Savior's breast," I can't help sometimes wondering how many really mean it. All right: Christian piety of another age can be altogether too sweet and sticky for our taste. But does that mean that we have to forget that the core of our faith remains a central love and loyalty to Jesus Christ? His final question in this Gospel is not: "Do you admire me?" nor "Are you busy in Christian causes?" nor "Do you find my philosophy attractive?" but just "Do you love me?" — and that love indicates nothing else than the total dedication of our lives to him.

To love in this sense means the gratitude and affection of one who knows that Christ has lived and died for him.

It means that Christ is the central point of reference in all the major decisions of our life. It means an increasing realization that the things he stands for matter more than anything else in the world. It means letting his Spirit more and more control the thoughts of our minds and the passions of our hearts. We hear a lot today about emptiness, the void in the soul, lack of purpose and direction. The fact is that everyone needs some dominant center to which, no matter how often we stray, we have to return; some integrating power to give direction to our scattered hopes and aspirations; some over-arching loyalty in which those other great loyalties of our life find their deepest meaning.

So Christ says to Peter: "Do you love me?" — and Peter here stands for you and me, and millions of people across the world who gather at the Lord's Table of Holy Communion. This is how I read the story. I don't think of it as an official recognition of Peter as leader of the church. When the Lord says: "Lovest thou me more than these?" I don't think he was asking from Peter a greater love than the other disciples were capable of giving. I believe the New English Bible is right in translating: "Do you love me more than all else?" The Lord is asking that same question of all his twentieth-century disciples. He knows that we live surrounded by an entrancing world of discovery and physical delights; that we are deeply concerned about the health of our bodies and the needs of our minds; that all kinds of good causes claim our attention and our time — and he says: "More than these? Really, do you love me more than these?"

The question is so searching that I for one am glad to think that it was Peter who had to answer it. For this was no plaster saint. This was the rough fisherman not given to making sentimental sounds about his religion. And this was a man who knew what it was to pledge loyalty and then miserably fail the test. "Lord," he had said at the last meal they had taken together, "I am ready to go with thee, both into prison and to death." And in a few hours he was cursing and swearing that he never knew the man. Three times he had denied, and in the infinite grace of our Lord Jesus Christ, three times he has now the chance to reaffirm his love. There's a whole gospel here — good news for those like you and me who are very conscious of disloyalty and failure, good news of another chance to say: "In spite of all that has drawn me away, in spite of my letting a hundred other things claim priority over my interest, my time, my money, my enthusiasm, I know that Christ matters most, that what he stands for is eternally right, that when this central loyalty is in good repair all else will fall into place." It's so human, isn't it? — and the response so divine. "You know that I love you: you know *everything*: you know I love you."

And that's where it ends? Is this the only loyalty-test: that we genuinely, humbly, contritely, confess our love for Christ? Is this the only point when we take Communion: that we receive the bread and wine as our way of saying, "You know that I love you"? If we think we can separate the inner devotion of our souls from the daily practice of Christian love, we don't know the Lord to whom we speak. He has no time for the devotion of the sanctuary that is not backed up by our action in the world. "Not every one that saith to me, Lord, Lord, shall enter into the kingdom of heaven: but he that doeth the will of my Father . . . ." As James put it: "What use is it for a man to say he has faith when he does nothing to show it? Suppose a brother or sister is in rags with not enough food for the day, and one of you says, 'Good luck to you, keep yourselves warm, and have plenty to eat,' but does nothing to supply their bodily needs, what is the good of that? So with faith, if it does not lead to action, it is in itself a lifeless thing."

"You know that I love you." "Then feed my lambs; tend my sheep." There's something quite unexpected in this brusque response. We tend to think of Christ accepting our devotion with the quiet smile you see on some of these sentimental paintings that decorate church halls. We would do better to have in mind a majestic Rembrandt or an agonizing El Greco as we listen to this "Feed my sheep." How easy it is to let these words fade into some peaceful pastoral scene in which St. Peter and the apostles shepherd the infant flock of Christians. Can we not hear the direct and urgent command that tests the loyalty of everyone who is willing to say: "Lord, I love you"? Sheep, lambs — that's men, women and children, whatever their race, whatever their color, whatever their religion, whatever their deserts. Feed them! They're hungry.

We begin with literal hunger, as Jesus did when he taught us to pray: "Give us — the whole human family — our daily bread." The bread is on our Communion table because our Lord wants us to see that faith in him, love for him, means not only sharing in a Holy Communion here, but sharing the staff of life with those who are starving. We know that today this same table is spread in places where a fragment of bread such as we take would represent real food. When we bring our offerings for dedication to God, surely some fraction of it must always go to the feeding of the hungry? I know that world hunger is an immense problem that leaves us often with no more Christian answer than a bad conscience, but there is always a giving to be done in the name of Christ. What we call our Missions and Benevolence section of the budget is not an optional interest but a loyalty-test. "Do you love me?" says Christ, "then feed my sheep." It's as simple — and as tough — as that.

Feed my sheep. Yes: feed their bodies. But there's more. Do you know that there are 700,000,000 in the world today who are illiterate? Feed their minds, says Christ. When he calls us sheep he does not mean that men are animals. Literacy is a Christian mission. And what will they read? Feed them, says Christ — surely "Feed them what will make them strong and healthy; feed them words of truth and beauty and hope. There will be others waiting to offer lies, and vice, and hatred. Feed them the Word of God."

"You love me?" says Christ, "then care about the people around you, beginning right where you are. Feed friendship to the lonely, hope to the discouraged, resources into every agency working against poverty and bad housing and disease. Feed new strength into the sagging hopes of men for justice, for peace, for freedom. Feed inspiration to the artist, laughter to the bored, happiness to the children. Feed, in every way you can, around this shrinking globe, the glory of my gospel: for I am come that they might have life, and have it more abundantly."

What is your picture of worldwide communion? Is it of a network of Christian huddles, each turned inwards to preserve the faith in a dangerous world, and deriving some faint comfort from the existence of the others? Could it not be of a universal church, united across the barriers and walls of our fractured humanity in a common love of Jesus Christ, breaking the same bread and drinking from the same cup, in order to penetrate this modern world with the Word and the works of healing for which it obviously hungers?

Of all the millions of Christians who worship today we are perhaps the most exposed to the corrosion of our faith by our comforts, and of our love by the sheer complexity of the society we live in. So we have special need to hear that question, "Do you love me more than all else?" And when we respond, "Yes, Lord, you know that I love you," are we ready to take the full weight of that final test, "Feed my sheep"? This is why he has brought us here — to renew our loyalty, to receive his strength, and to know again what it is to be a member, a living member, in his universal church.

18. *Our Most Rampant Sin*

Wherefore he saith,
Awake thou that sleepest,
and arise from the dead,
and Christ shall give thee
light. EPHESIANS 5:14

It's not often these days that you will see on a church notice-board, or advertised in the newspapers, a sermon topic containing the word "Sin." Yet the word can hardly be said to be unpopular today, since you will find it quite frequently on the marquees, and the advertising, of more squalid movie-houses in our large cities. It begins to look as though a word that the churches are avoiding, because it sounds negative and disapproving, has been picked up by the pornographers because it sounds sexy and exciting.

I hope it won't disappoint anyone when I say that the sin I am going to speak about this morning has little, if anything, to do with sex. Sin, according to the Shorter Catechism, is "any want of conformity unto, or transgression of, the law of God." In other words, it means not living up to, or actually violating, the design of God for our lives. For those who want a still simpler definition we could say that sin is the evil in the world, the wrong in our lives, that is *our own fault.* We have just lived through an era when every effort was made to eliminate the idea that anything could be our own fault. We were encouraged to place the blame on our ancestors, our glands, our environment, our unconscious, or even the laws of nature. Now I believe we are a little more ready to admit that there is such a thing as a voluntary choice of what is wrong, a failure in goodness for which we are responsible. If we believe in God, then there is no other name for this wrongdoing, this wrong thinking, this failure, than sin.

I know that there is much confusion in our minds as to what is wrong, and as to what exactly IS the good life we so often fail to reach. It isn't as if what we call "the law of God" is so minutely codified that we can consult the book and find out exactly what our transgressions are. Yet surely we have sufficient light from the Bible, the Christian tradition, and above all from the character of Jesus Christ, to be able to distinguish certain acts, certain habits of mind, as sinful. In fact many of us have experienced the paradox that the closer we come to Jesus Christ the more we are conscious of our sins. So why should we hesitate to spotlight certain habits and tendencies and call them what they are — sins?

It's anybody's guess as to which sin is most rampant in our society, which sin is most indulged by Christian people — and it doesn't really matter, except by way of putting us on our guard. From a knowledge of myself, from what other people have confessed to me, and from a certain mood that infects both church and society today, I have come to the conclusion that one particular sin has a terrible grip on most of us, weakens our Christian character, and enervates society. The odd thing is that this most prevalent of sins has no one name that you would immediately recognize. The only name that I can find is one that was used in the Middle Ages and still survives in our dictionaries. It was listed in those days with the other six "deadly sins" — pride, covetousness, lust, anger, envy, and gluttony. And its name was *accidie.* That's what I want to talk about.

You will find that in most lists of the deadly sins it appears as sloth, or laziness. But this is only one symptom of a much more subtle and complex sin. The word "accidie" or "acedia" comes from the Greek *akedos,* meaning "not caring." If there was one English word like "couldn't-care-lessishness" it would come much nearer to what is meant by this sin than sloth. But it is even more complex than this. So instead of playing word-games let me offer some examples of this sin, and see if you recognize them.

When we are dealing with fundamental recesses of the human heart it is fascinating to note how little human beings change in spite of the enormous differences in conditions of life. Thus we find that, although we should not dream of consulting the ancients for reliable scientific information, the moral insights of a Socrates, an Isaiah, a Paul, a Dante, or a Shakespeare are as valid today as when they were first expressed. I can hardly think of anyone further away from modern Manhattan than a fourth-century monk. Yet listen to this description that Cassian, who founded monasteries in Palestine and southern France around 500 B.C., gives of a monk who gives way to accidie:

"When the poor fellow is beset by it, it makes him detest the place where he is, and loathe his cell; and he has a poor and scornful opinion of his brethren, near and far, and thinks that they are neglectful and unspiritual. It makes him sluggish and inert for every task; he cannot sit still, nor give his mind to reading; he thinks despondently how little progress he has made where he is, how little good he gains or does . . . he dwells much on the excellence of other and distant monasteries; he thinks how profitable and healthy life is there; how delightful the brethren are, and how spiritually they talk. On the contrary, where he is, all seems harsh and untoward; there is no refreshment for his soul to be got from his brethren, and none for his body from the thankless land. At last he thinks he really cannot be saved if he stops where he is; and then, about eleven or twelve o'clock, he feels as tired as if he had walked miles, and as hungry as if he had fasted for two or three days. He goes out and looks this way and that, and sighs to think that there is no one coming to visit him; he saunters to and fro, and wonders why the sun is setting so slowly; and so, with his mind full of stupid bewilderment and shameful gloom, he grows slack and void of all spiritual energy, and thinks that nothing will do him any good save to go and call on somebody, or else to betake himself to the solace of sleep." That's accidie in action — or rather inaction.

(Once when I was chaplain in a prison camp where one is especially subject to this sin, I quoted this passage in a sermon — and was accused afterwards of having made it all up!)

St. John of Damascus, in the eighth century, has this definition of accidie: "a sorrowfulness so weighing down the mind that there is no good it likes to do. It has attached to it as its inseparable comrade a distress and weariness of soul, and a sluggishness in all good works, which plunges the whole man into lazy languor, and works in him a constant bitterness."

Dante deals with accidie in his great poem, locating the milder form — laziness and lukewarmness — in the "Purgatorio," and the more serious form — sullenness, gloom, and anger — in the "Inferno." Those who still can read Chaucer will find a brilliant description of accidie in the "Parson's Tale" of which it is the subject. Every sensitive writer in the Christian tradition has shown some recognition of this sin. It may be anonymous but I doubt if there is anyone here who has escaped its attack.

I should make it clear that we are not talking about the kind of morbid depression that is the result of physical or mental illness. In such cases, of course, medical help is called for rather than talk of sin. I am speaking of the moods that come over a normally healthy Christian man or woman, moods which we are tempted to indulge rather than resist. Don't we all know, in varying degrees, that grey mood that settles on the soul, when nothing seems really worth doing, when meaning drains out of life, when we find it hard to respond with real interest to things we care most about, when we tend to despair of ever being better or stronger characters than we are now, and to take a cynical view of people around, of mankind in general? I suspect that many of us imagine that the really energetic people we know, especially those who are animated by a strong Christian faith, are immune to any such moods. The God "unto whom all hearts are open, all desires known, and from whom no secrets are hid" I am sure knows otherwise. Accidie strikes at the most unexpected people at unexpected times and places. The sin is not that it comes, but in our glum and unresisting acceptance of the mood.

The symptoms of accidie are all over the place. Why do we not react as once we would to stories of injustice, cruelty, and distress? Why is there such acquiescence in cynical slogans such as: "You'll never abolish war"; "New York is ungovernable"; "You'll never get the churches together"; "Everyone is out for himself"? Why do so many books and plays reflect a stale amorality of outlook, so singularly devoid of compassion? What lies behind the current surge of satire and sick jokes, in which nothing whatever is held sacred any more? Why is it so difficult to get volunteers for jobs to be done in the community and quality candidates for public office? Why are we so often listless and languid about causes in which we really believe — like the mission of the Christian church? Why is there so often a dullness in our prayers and a lack of lively expectation in our worship? Accidie at work — that's what it is. It's one of the more subtle sins because it doesn't come in the form of sudden passion, or flagrant denial of our faith. It simply draws a grey shadow over all that we really believe and care about, leaving our faith apparently intact but actually lifeless and inert. If we fall into one of the more familiar sins we may, by God's grace, experience the shock of confession and forgiveness, but this sin nibbles away at the soul and we hardly notice that it is destroying the hope and joy and trust and compassion that are the essence of our Christian faith.

Enough of analysis. What are our resources for dealing with this sin?

When St. Paul wrote to the Ephesian Church he had in mind this non-caring lassitude of the spirit. We so often think of the early Christians as tremendously energetic, active people, continually risking their lives in Christ's service, that it is something of a shock to hear the apostle warning them against accidie. For that is surely behind his exhortations to wake up, to redeem the time, and to be filled with the Spirit. He reminds them of a hymn that had been composed with this sin in mind. The words "wherefore he saith" usually introduce a quotation from the Old Testament. But the words of our text are not to be found there. They are surely from a popular hymn of the first-century church. And this is the only line that has been preserved: "Awake thou that sleepest, and arise from the dead, and Christ shall give thee light."

Singing itself is a great remedy for accidie, as men have often discovered in times of danger and depression — not only in church. But these words convey something much more than this advice about "speaking to yourselves in psalms and hymns and spiritual songs, singing and making melody in our heart to the Lord."

"Awake thou that sleepest, and arise from the dead." Just as every one of us knows the kind of morning when it would be so easy, so pleasant, so comfortable to lie another hour or two in bed, but somehow manages to summon up the will power to throw off the blankets, so it is surely possible when accidie comes sneaking up with its suggestion that nothing really matters too much, with its cloud of unattached depression and listlessness of spirit, to meet it with at least as much effort of the will. "Awake thou that sleepest, and arise from the dead" — you can hear these words at such a moment — not just as a hearty slap on the back, but as a solemn reminder that surrender to accidie is spiritual death. The resurrection power of Christ is not only a demonstration that physical death has been conquered and the gates of eternal life thrown open to all believers. It is available here and now to raise us from the apathy and despair that are the death of the soul.

In practice this usually means that the best answer to accidie is to get to work. We all know that in times of idleness or unemployment we are more liable to succumb to accidie than when we are busy. But there is no time when there is not something quite practical and necessary to do. The choice is open to us. We can let the mood settle on us — or we can thumb our nose at accidie and get on with the job. I have always been fascinated by the story of Elijah just after he had had the tremendous showdown with the prophets of Baal. Often it is just after such a moment of exaltation that we are most susceptible to an attack of accidie. It certainly happened to Elijah. He heard that Queen Jezebel was out for his blood and took off. And this is what we read: "he himself went a day's journey into the wilderness, and came and sat down under a juniper tree: and he requested for himself that he might die: and said, It is enough; now, O Lord, take away my life; for I am not better than my fathers."

There it is, despair, blank depression, abandonment of all hope for better things. The voice of the angel comes: "Arise and eat." He summons up the energy to do just that, then a little later back comes accidie for another attack. "And he came thither to a cave, and lodged there; and, behold, the word of the Lord came to him, and he said unto him, What doest thou here, Elijah?" Have you ever heard that voice when you were in the cave of accidie? It's the beginning of the cure when we really hear it. "What doest thou here?" "And he said, I have been very jealous for the Lord God of hosts; for the children of Israel have forsaken thy covenant, thrown down thine altars, and slain thy prophets with the sword; and I, even I only, am left; and they seek my life to take it away." Then came the strong wind, and the earthquake — and finally the still small voice. But accidie still has Elijah in its grip. Again comes his pathetic complaint — accidie knows how to use self-pity — "I, even I only, am left: and they seek my life to take it away." "And the Lord said unto him, Go, return on thy way to the wilderness of Damascus. . . ." Here he is in the cave of accidie, utterly defeated, totally depressed. "And the Lord said, Go!" In just this kind of way, in our own small crises, or even serious despair, the word of the Lord may be just this: "Go! Get on with it!"

Another old saint, known as St. John of the Ladder, has a treatise in which the voice of accidie is heard, speaking like this. "They who summon me are many; sometimes it is dullness and senselessness of soul that bids me come, sometimes it is forgetfulness of things above; aye, and there are times when it is excess of toil. My adversaries are the singing of psalms and the labor of the hands; the thought of death is my enemy, *but that which kills me outright is prayer.*

To meet the attack of accidie with prayer means more than just a quick appeal to God to drive away the black mood. For if we really set ourselves to prayer at such a time, all kinds of things begin to happen. Right away we are beginning to rise from the dead; for whenever we honestly turn our thoughts to God new life begins to flow. The promise is realized: Christ shall give thee light. The light will fall on the landscape that had begun to look so bleak. We shall be reminded again that the great purpose of God is still at work, even though for us it seems to have come for the moment to a standstill. The light will fall on the people around us, with whom we live and work. We shall begin to care for them again. The light will fall on this person and on that, who have far more to bear than we, and our petty troubles begin to recede. The light will fall on the hopes and aspirations that have grown dull and dim, and we shall know again that there is a better life within our reach, an endless possibility of being more like Christ.

And the light will fall, sooner or later, on that central symbol of our Christian faith — the cross where the Son of God agonized for us all. We have heard listed the common sins that brought him to that terrible death. Don't you think accidie was among them? As well as the active agents of hate, and fear, of expediency and politics, that led to the crucifixion, was there not a great mass of sheer torpor and indifference, the shoulder-shrugging of men who "could not care less"? I don't believe that any one of us could spend a true moment of prayer and meditation in the presence of that cross, thinking: "This, *this,* is what God means to me" — a love that gives everything, a compassion that goes the whole way through the valley of the shadow, a new hope born into the world as the sin and suffering are absorbed in a death which destroys the power of death, and a new life promised that grows towards an eternal fulfillment — without finding our spirits renewed, our hopes revived, and the shadow of accidie slinking back to the hell from whence it came.

From that little church in Ephesus, nineteen centuries ago, where Christians met who had much more reason to despair, to give up their hopes for themselves or their church or their world, much more reason to cease to care than we, I hear a song. It has never ceased to sound in Christian hearts, alone or in company, in every land. And it reaches us today as the Word of the living God: "Awake thou that sleepest, and arise from the dead, and Christ shall give thee light."

19. *Really Radical Religion*

And now I will show you the best way of all. . . . I CORINTHIANS 12:31 (NEB)

This summer I read a letter in a weekly magazine written by a distinguished British politician on the subject of religion. In it he advanced the rather dusty theory, spawned in nineteenth-century Germany and brilliantly popularized by George Bernard Shaw, that the religion of St. Paul was totally different from the religion of Jesus. It would be tempting to press upon him the scholarly works of the last fifty years in which this theory has been demolished. But it would be much simpler to ask if he had ever read the thirteenth chapter of the first epistle to the Corinthians. It is surely impossible to hear these words without recognizing at once who it is that has inspired them. They breathe the very spirit of the Christ we find in the Gospels; they echo his words, and they bring us into his presence. In fact it is in Christ alone that this portrait of love has been fully realized.

We hear a lot today about radical religion. The term is used to indicate a radical break with the past — an "agonizing reappraisal" of our beliefs and practices in the Christian church, leading to a new version of Christianity in tune with the spirit of the times. That some changes — even radical changes — are necessary most alert Christians will be ready to admit. But let me remind you what "radical" really means. It is not just a synonym for "advanced," "ultramodern," "far-out," or "extremely progressive." It means "getting to the roots." And getting to the roots is the very opposite of what is often implied by the use of "radical" today. We think of a radical politician as one who wants to cut loose from the heritage of the past, a radical artist as one who has broken with the traditions of his craft, a radical theologian as one who has wiped aside the ancient creeds of the church. The real "radical" is the one who goes to the roots. He wants to get at the living center, and base his life and his opinions on what he finds there.

Such a process often means upheaval. For in the course of time any vital movement acquires a vast overgrowth, a luxuriant foliage in which it is easy to get lost. Christianity, for instance, means a lot of different things to us today — a religious experience, a church, a code of morals, a charitable organization, a philosophy, a social action group, a friendly society, a set of doctrines. Sometimes it seems so complicated, so overgrown, so tangled that we long for some kind of defoliation. Radical religion seeks the real roots, the basic essential — and is prepared for the upheaval that such a search may mean.

It occurred to me recently, when thinking about these things, that there is no more radical religion than that which is set out in this chapter. It goes to the roots of our faith. It presents us with the living center, which is nothing else than the love that is here described. Without this nothing is truly radical in any of the movements that agitate the church today. Without this we can have all the foliage of religion but lack its root. And with this — grasped again as the central challenge to your life and mine — the most radical revolution of all takes place in us, in our church, in our society, and in the world.

This chapter comes right in the middle of a letter that deals with all kinds of problems, debates, movements, and confused ideas that were swirling in the Corinthian Church. It is not difficult to find their equivalents in the church today. St. Paul deals patiently, wisely, sometimes quite sharply with the various groups that were sounding off in the early church. He appreciates what all were trying to do, and continually underlines the fact that God expects a great diversity of gifts and temperaments in his community of Christians on earth. Then suddenly, as if the Spirit had really gripped his pen, he says: "And now I will show you the best way of all." Back to the roots. Here is the living center. This is what matters more than anything else. Don't you think that God wants to break into our confusions, our debates, our conflicting interests and enthusiasms, in just the same way? "I will show you the best way of all."

In three short paragraphs he tells of the supremacy, the nature, and the permanence of love. The immortal beauty of the passage, especially in our King James Version, has made it part of the heritage of the English-speaking world. But, for that very reason, we may miss the flow of the reasoning, the power of the presentation, and the radical challenge that is offered to our way of life. Above all we may miss the hidden premise that directs his thought: that such love is no human technique for living, but is revealed, and made possible, by the God who "so loved the world that he gave his Son."

The first paragraph speaks of the *supremacy* of love. Paul lists four activities of Christians that are normally considered supremely important, or — if you like — four movements in the church that tend to claim priority, and he boldly says that without love they are nothing. It's not difficult to translate these movements from the context of the Corinthian Church to the present day.

"I may speak in tongues of men or of angels." The immediate reference is to those who had what is called the gift of tongues, or "glossolalia." This is the religion of ecstasy. Under the impulse of an intense time of prayer Christians would break out into strange languages. Those who had this gift tended to feel that they belonged to the elite of the church. This was the real sign that God was at work among them. Nothing mattered more than to have the whole church share in this experience of ecstasy. As you know this particular phenomenon exists today, not only in Pentecostal churches but in unexpected quarters among the more conventional churches. But we can surely extend the thought here to all highly charged, emotional experience of the gospel. There are those among us today who feel that no Christian experience is valid without their ecstatic experience of conversion, or their emotional response to the Bible message. What the apostle says is: "Fine, thank God if you have this experience of ecstasy; but remember that it is not the root of the gospel. Love comes first — and it is horribly possible to indulge your religious emotion without love. Ecstasy without love is like the meaningless music of a gong or a cymbal — boom, boom, boom! clang, clang, clang!" In a phrase the apostle pins down a type of Christian who haunts the church in every age — the one who can indulge in an orgy of religious emotion while remaining selfish and unloving in the practical affairs of every day.

"I may have the gift of prophecy, and know every hidden truth." This time he has in mind not the ecstatic, but the intellectual. The gift of prophecy, in modern terms, is the capacity to analyze, to criticize, to denounce contemporary trends, to indicate better ways for the church: and with it goes the theological passion for knowing "every hidden truth." St. Paul himself was a prophet, and had an insatiable appetite for theological exploration. He knew the importance for the church of men and women who trained their minds on the problems of the day, and pursued truth with single-minded zeal. The intellectual is as valuable in the church as the ecstatic. In American Protestantism today there is desperate need for the prophetic voice, for the penetrating mind, for a higher level of theological thought.

Yet here again comes the devastating reminder: "If I have no love, I am nothing." If the sin of the ecstatic is intolerance and spiritual pride, the sin of the intellectual is arrogance and mental pride. Ecstasy without love is a boom and a tinkle; intellect without love is — nothing, emptiness that is left when everything is criticized, and exploration goes round in circles without ever resting in God.

Now comes faith. Surely, we think, this is the Christian virtue par excellence — the faith that our Lord continually commended, the faith that consists in an overwhelming sense of God's presence and power. Yet what are we told? With an obvious reference to a saying of our Lord, the apostle boldly affirms: "I may have faith strong enough to move mountains; but if I have no love, I am nothing." This seems a shocker: *faith,* terrific faith, and yet — nothing? Do you remember once when Jesus and his disciples had had a rough reception in a village they suggested to him that he call down fire on it, like Elisha? That was faith, faith that he had indeed such power. But what was his reply? "Ye know not what spirit ye are of." In their feverish faith they had forgotten the spirit of Christ, which is the spirit of love. And at that moment they were as nothing in his sight — useless, empty, totally profitless servants. Sometimes in our concentration upon faith we may be deluded into thinking that nothing else matters than an increasing conviction in the power of God to work through us, forgetting that the only faith that matters is the faith that works through love. This is why we are directed to make our prayers "through Jesus Christ our Lord." When we mean these words we are delivered from the kind of prayer that simply wants God's power revealed. Great faith could pray: "Lord, destroy all the enemies of the church, all the enemies of my country," but not the faith that knows the supremacy of love. For we cannot pray such a prayer "through Jesus Christ our Lord." Faith is essential, but love remains supreme.

Now comes the climactic statement, the most astonishing contrast of all. Surely if there is a supreme Christian virtue it is that of total giving of one's possessions and oneself. In fact we have often been taught that this *is* Christian love — to give one's goods for others, to offer even the supreme sacrifice of life itself for Christ's sake. Yet look at what is written: "I may dole out all I possess, or even give my body to be burnt, but if I have no love, I am none the better."

This love we are studying, this love we seek to know in our lives, must be something more than what has seemed to us the greatest possible demonstration of self-giving. And when we stop to think about it we shall realize that it *is* possible to be intensely active in the service of our fellow men without the inspiration and guidance of love: it *is* possible even to be a martyr for Christ's sake and lack the spirit of love that animated the Lord himself. We are being reminded that social action — whether that of the man who contributes most generously to good causes, or the one who is immersed in the battle to win justice and freedom for others, or the one who is willing to put everything on the line for what he believes — can lack the one great Christian motive, the one great Christian grace. "To give of one's substance" — as we promise in our vows of church membership — can be a joyful activity of Christian love; but it can also be just a grim duty, or even a cause for self-congratulation. To plunge into Christian action for the righting of social wrongs can be a glorious expression of faith and love; or it can be a kind of partisan enterprise, of zeal without love. Even a martyr, says the apostle, could lack this love — and "be none the better." This seems a hard saying but he must have known the fanaticism that could be utterly loveless.

Ecstasy, intellect, faith, self-giving — all these are among the greatest Christian gifts, but without the supreme gift they are nothing. And what is that supreme gift?

I can do no more than let you hear again the nature of love, let you see again the portrait of love in action. For it *is* action. Although the new translation is closer to the Greek the King James Version has the virtue of preserving the verbs. For St. Paul did not describe love in adjectives; and we can hear the action, the warm, breathing life that lies behind his words. You might, in fact, go through this chapter replacing the word "love" or "charity" by "Christ," and scene after scene from the Gospels will flash before your eyes.

"Christ is patient; Christ is kind and envies no one. Christ is never boastful, nor conceited, nor rude; never selfish, not quick to take offense. Christ keeps no score of wrongs; does not gloat over other men's sins, but delights in the truth. There is nothing Christ cannot face; there is no limit to his faith, his hope, and his endurance."

Then comes the mighty reason for the supremacy of this love. "Love will never come to an end." If we think of love as a mere decoration in our lives, or as a passing experience of human life, we have not heard the tremendous assurance of the gospel. "Love never ends." It is, as Henry Drummond put it, "the greatest thing in the world," because it alone of all the great qualities of the human spirit, of all the graces of the Christian life, endures into eternity. Prophecy is for this world only; ecstasy as we know it now will be transformed in the life eternal; knowledge will vanish away. All these things are partial, temporary, and destined to be swallowed up "when wholeness comes."

Since this is not too easy for us to grasp, the apostle here puts in two illustrations. First he compares what happens to our present knowledge to what happens to our childish ideas once we have grown up. In eternity even the most profound wisdom we have acquired, the most brilliant discoveries we have made, will seem like infant prattling compared with the knowledge that will flow to us from the very presence of God. Then he likens our present understanding to "puzzling reflections in a mirror." (We have to think here, not of our modern brilliant reflectors, but of the dim burnished metal which was what they used at the time.) The best of our knowledge now is only partial. (We might remember that this includes all our creeds, our confessions and our theologies.) In God's actual presence it will be whole — like his knowledge of us now.

What he is saying is that the other gifts, great as they are, cannot be eternal, for all will be swallowed up, or transformed in the conditions of eternity. I believe the King James Version has the better reading for the last verse. "*Now* abideth faith, hope, and charity." Something similar to faith may last into the eternal world; something there may be still to hope for; but there is only one grace that is absolute, enduring, and ultimate. "The greatest of them all is love."

So ends the great exposition of the supremacy, the nature, and the permanence of love. But it cannot come to an end on the printed page. The only point of studying it is that it may leave the Bible to become incarnate in the lives of people like you and me. We are not here to analyze love, but to know it, and to live it. We are not here to study a doctrine, but to be infected by a life. For it is a life that lies behind the inspired words of the apostle — the life of Jesus Christ. What made him certain of the supremacy of love? Christ, who revealed that this is the very nature of the God we worship. What inspired his description of the nature of love? Christ, who displayed it in life and death. What made him so sure of the permanence of love? Christ, who after giving himself to the uttermost for men is now "most high in the glory of God the Father." The one hope we have, as struggling mortals in a world of confusion, of passions, hates, and discord, of being infused with any of this supreme and eternal quality of love, is to be yielded to the mastery of Christ our Lord. One thing we know: Love, this love, is the one way of life that can never be wrong. In our faith, our knowledge, our ecstasies we can make terrible mistakes. But every act that conforms to this picture of love is eternally right.

20. *Christ and the Misfit*

And he ran before, and climbed up into a sycamore tree to see him: for he was to pass that way. And when Jesus came to the place, he looked up, and saw him, and said unto him, Zacchaeus, make haste, and come down; for today I must abide at thy house.
LUKE 19:4-5

Zacchaeus was a misfit. There was little that was normal about him — neither his occupation, his habits, his income, nor even his height. As a Jew, he worked for the Romans; and his work was eccentric and unpopular since he was a tax-collector. He wasn't asked out to dinner by his neighbors, and didn't feel himself very welcome at the synagogue. In income he was well above normal, and in stature well below. In this one story that has survived about him he is the odd man out in the Jericho crowd. So when Jesus passed through the city on his last journey to Jerusalem and a mob surged around to catch a glimpse of the young prophet about whom so many stories were circulating, Zacchaeus had to use the familiar technique of the small boy who wants to see. He climbed a tree.

Let's leave him there for a while. We'll come back to this misfit on his tree before this sermon is done. I want now to switch to another picture, much more familiar to you. You'll see it in magazines from time to time, on billboards, or in buses. In the front pew of a nice clean church stand a shining family — Mr. and Mrs. Normal and their three normal children. They are nicely, but not too expensively dressed. They look devout, but not too devout. They are singing a hymn, but not too enthusiastically. Mr. and Mrs. Normal obviously fell in love at the proper time, had their children at correct intervals, and have no serious problems in their married life. They would obviously be acceptable guests in any normal home, desirable members for any average club. Their opinions on current affairs are those of what politicians like to describe as "right-thinking men and women." They can obviously eat without gaining weight, and drink without becoming alcoholics. Their children are going to grow up, passing the right examinations at the right time, making the right kind of friends, perfectly adjusted to the society of normal people. And, of course, they carry life insurance — but not too much. So there they are at worship, without a worry in the world: and of such, thinks the man in the street today, is the church of Jesus Christ.

This is part of the mythology of modern America — first: that there exists such a family that is so completely normal; second — and this worries me much more — that the church is around to bless this normality and inspire the rest of us to reach this goal. I believe that this myth is responsible for a lot of unhappiness as real, flesh-and-blood human beings measure themselves up against the normal family and conclude that they are misfits, and for a lot of sham and costly pretense as others put on a show of such normality. We are haunted by the pretty picture and feel guilty if our lives don't quite fit the pattern. If we brood long enough on the difference between our experience and this model family we may despair, and head for the nearest psychiatrist. Or we may buy a new suit or dress, sprinkle on the latest lotion, borrow some money, and pass ourselves off as well on the way to being normal people. How much better it would be if we just kicked Mr. and Mrs. Normal back into the limbo where they belong, and frankly faced the fact that we are all just sinful, struggling, hopeful, half-fulfilled, half-frustrated, plus and minus men and women, each with our quirks and oddities, our own unique experience of the rough and tumble of human existence.

It especially bothers me that this myth of the normal family hangs around the church. In sermons and prayers and hymns the impression is often given that our pews are filled with normal families whose smooth passage through life needs just a passing boost from the church. We give the impression that the vast majority of church members fit into the conventional pattern, and their prayers and compassion are asked for the few misfits — the unhappy, the deprived, the bereaved — as the Bible puts it, "the poor, and the maimed, and the halt, and the blind." It's time we woke up to who we really are. In the first place, the truth is that a large proportion of an average congregation is unmarried, widowed, divorced, or childless, and have no chance of conforming to the pattern of Mr. and Mrs. Normal. More important still, there is not one of us who has not some frustration, some private worry, some secret battle, some twist of character, or some agonizing experience that seems to shut us off from this happy picture of normality. Let's face it; if there is such a thing as normality we're all misfits.

The damage that is done if we insist on the myth of normality is incalculable. For it leaves many feeling inside that they are not quite the right type of person. They are left with the impression that they don't really belong in a society of thoroughly healthy, normal Christians. Isn't it an enormous relief to learn that you are just as abnormal as the man or woman in the next pew — and even more, that they are just as abnormal as you? Too often the church member lives under the strain of thinking that he alone is the odd man out, and that he must strive towards an impossible ideal. And on the people outside the church this myth may well be the one great deterrent that keeps them well away from any thought of membership. We have succeeded too often in projecting an image of the church of Christ that has far more in common with the picture of the normal family than with Zacchaeus.

Why are there so many people within a short radius around the typical church who never dream of entering it for worship — or anything else? I am thinking of the thousands who have no kind of church connection, but exactly the same needs as the rest of us, and similar hopes and anxieties. May it not be because they feel instinctively that this is not their kind of place? Somewhere there hovers around the myth of the normal Christian family and they feel they don't belong — or, more likely still, they want no part of it. It is tragic that so many think of the church today as a group of the religious-minded, playing happy families rather than as a fellowship of misfits being shaped and molded by the grace of God. For that is what we truly are.

Our Lord made this perfectly clear from the beginning. "I am not come to call the righteous," he said, "but sinners to repentance." You can hear the quotes around "righteous" as he speaks, for he knew that the "righteous" are like the mythical normal family. They don't exist. God did not send his Son to confer a blessing on people whose lives were flowing smoothly, and for whom no problems loomed larger than a cold in the head. He came "to seek and to save that which is lost" — and the lost are precisely those who know that they are not normal, that they do not automatically belong in the company of the smooth and satisfied. Do you think that Christ would have gone through the agony of crucifixion on behalf of normal people who only need an occasional pat on the back to keep them on the smooth path of happiness and success? It was "while we were yet sinners" — twisted, maimed, and abnormal, misfits in the paradise of God — that Christ died for us. The gospel is good news because it is pointed straight at one who knows himself to be off-base, who is aware of his isolation, and offers to bring him into the company, not of the normal, but of the crooked who are being straightened out — or, as the Bible would say, sinners who are being saved.

The Bible is a continually surprising book. When I began to wonder where I might find in it the words to fit the picture of Mr. and Mrs. Normal, I came across this in the book of Job: "Their seed is established in their sight with them, and their offspring before their eyes. Their houses are safe from fear, neither is the rod of God upon them. Their bull gendereth, and faileth not; their cow calveth, and casteth not her calf. [Today we would read: "their investment gendereth and faileth not; and there are two cars in their garage."] They send forth their little ones like a flock, and their children dance. They take the timbrel and harp, and rejoice at the sound of the organ. [You've seen that family in the advertisements.] They spend their days in wealth, and in a moment go down to the grave."

And whom is Job describing? The words are introduced by: "Wherefore do the wicked live?" Job is answering his friends who were telling him what a misfit he was and how he must have offended God to have suffered such calamities. They painted the picture of the normal life that God blesses. "Normal nothing," says Job in effect, "that's the wicked you're describing." For he perceived beneath the outward prosperity the hollowness of those who do not know how poor they really are. At the other end of the Bible one of the letters in the Revelation makes the same point. "Because thou sayest, I am rich, and increased with goods, and have need of nothing; and knowest not that thou art wretched, and miserable, and poor, and blind, and naked; I counsel thee to buy of me gold tried in the fire . . . ." It is those who know that they are sick who go to the doctor, said Jesus, and it was the sick he came to cure. You might say that the only ones who are excluded from the church he came to found, from the kingdom he announced, are those who imagine they are too normal to require the healing grace of God.

When that man in the parable threw a big party and sent out invitations, his guests were too busy to come. They were all absorbed in normal activities — business and family life. "I have bought a piece of ground, and I must needs go and see it; I pray thee have me excused." "I have bought five yoke of oxen, and I go to prove them; I pray thee have me excused." "I have married a wife, and therefore I cannot come." So what happened? "Go out quickly into the streets and lanes of the city, and bring in hither the poor, and the maimed, and the halt, and the blind." This is the Lord's picture of his church. Those who fit in smoothly to the normal way of life, and feel no need to any radical change, are not to be found at his table. It is spread for the "poor, and the maimed, and the halt, and the blind." In other words God sends his Son to the misfits, to those who realize that they have a special need.

Let's look again at Zacchaeus, up that tree. The crowd

is surging beneath him, struggling and pushing to get a glimpse of Jesus as he went through the town. There is probably not much more in that crowd than average, normal curiosity. You might expect Jesus to seize the opportunity to make what we would call a whistle-stop speech. Perhaps Zacchaeus from his tree is expecting just that. Instead the eyes of Christ pass across that huge crowd, and then are raised to the leafy branches of a single tree. And Zacchaeus, the misfit, finds himself caught in the steady and penetrating gaze of the Son of God. "When Jesus came to the place, he looked up, and saw him, and said unto him, Zacchaeus, make haste, and come down; for today I must abide at thy house."

We never really hear the gospel till we realize that this is how Christ meets us. We may think it is some general message of goodwill to the world, or that it is the prerequisite of normal religious people. In fact it comes right to each of us at the point of our deepest need, where we are most conscious of our alienation from our fellows and from God. In a true service of Christian worship the gospel is not sprayed over a group of like-minded people as a kind of holy scent. It comes like an arrow to each individual heart, an arrow of love, of mercy, and of healing. It is as if Christ sought out each one of us, knowing all about the very things that make us feel awkward and ashamed, and said: "Today I must abide at *thy* house." The gospel is for you, and for me, just when we most feel ourselves to be misfits.

And what happens? Does the end of the story, that the encounter with Christ does finally make us all normal, bring us into that picture of the standard happy family which we have rejected as a myth? Let's look at the record of what happened to Zacchaeus.

There's nothing to indicate that this man immediately became a popular figure, "one of the boys." In fact the crowd objected that Christ "was gone to be a guest with a man that is a sinner." Zacchaeus was still going to be odd man out in quite a lot of ways. And there is certainly no miracle worked to bring him up to normal height! As a follower of Christ Zacchaeus would be a little man to the end of his days. Nor was he asked, like the rich young ruler, to divest himself of all his wealth. He would still have the weight, the worry, the responsibility that great wealth brings.

The New Testament shows a huge variety of character and temperament in the service of Christ. There is no standardized, model Christian disciple. And we have no reason to suppose that all the special quirks or disabilities that are ours to bear will be eliminated by our faith in Christ. There are some things setting us apart from the normal which he simply teaches us to accept. He does not expect to have a church composed entirely of happy families. How many of the great saints of the past or the present are what you might call normal people, sharing all the fulfillments and satisfactions for which men seek? Christ looks up at Zacchaeus and says: "I want you as you are; and I will teach you to live with yourself."

But — there is an area of life where the entrance of the Son of God brings a liberating and transforming power. There are immense changes to be wrought in the inner man by the friendship of the living Christ. A man, as Jesus said, cannot by hard thinking add a cubit to his height; but he can be raised to new stature as a moral being. He may not have his physical disabilities removed, or be able to escape from an evil chain of circumstances, but he can be given new faith and courage to live with his limitations. He may not be able to win popularity, but he can know the joy of obedience to a newly awakened conscience. This is what happened to Zacchaeus. The very first result of his encounter with Christ was the healing of his crafty and avaricious soul. "And Zacchaeus stood, and said unto the Lord; Behold, Lord, the half of my goods I give to the poor; and if I have taken any thing from any man by false accusation [that "if" shows that the cure was not complete, for he knew very well he had!], I restore him fourfold."

The Lord had met the misfit. To the end of his days, like you and me, he would always be some kind of a misfit. But he now knew the amazing truth that God is concerned above all with the peculiarities of each of his sons and daughters. And he experienced immediately the healing of God's grace at the very point where real change was needed. "And Jesus said unto him, This day is salvation come to this house."

Salvation. You see, it's not a peculiar something that is sung about by normal religious people. It is a spiritual revolution with practical results that occurs in the lives of us misfits when we drop the barriers and surrender to the grace of our Lord Jesus Christ, and the love of God, and the fellowship of the Holy Spirit. This is the gospel by which we live as a Christian congregation, and this is the gospel we have to bring not to a mass, not to anonymous "modern man" — but to each, unique, individual, fundamentally non-normal man, woman, and child within our reach today.

21. *God's New Protestants*

And think not to say within yourselves, We have Abraham to our father; for I say unto you, that God is able of these stones to raise up children unto Abraham. MATTHEW 3:9

There are estimated to be 224 million Protestants in the world today. Where are all these Protestants? Well, there are more of them in the U.S.A. than there are adherents of any other faith. In Europe they are in the majority in Britain, the Scandinavian countries, Germany, Switzerland and — barely — in Holland. Canada, Australia, New Zealand, and other Commonwealth countries are predominantly Protestant: and there are strong minorities in France, Hungary, South America, and some of the African and Asian lands.

Who are these people who are officially classed as Protestants? It would be hard to find a common denominator. They range from Episcopalians to Holy Rollers, from Calvinists to Christian Scientists, from Quakers to Pentecostals. I suspect that many let themselves be listed as Protestants for no other reason than that they are not Roman Catholics. There is, however, a mainstream of Protestant tradition, deriving from Luther and Calvin, that nourishes what we call our Protestant heritage today. Something happened in the sixteenth century that we call the Reformation and it had a decisive effect on the history of the world. The nations most affected by it have been, on the whole, the dominant and most dynamic peoples of the last five hundred years. The energies released by the Reformation probably more than anything else created modern civilization, and, until recent years, determined its course. So those who today are listed in the world census as Protestants are the inheritors of a mighty tradition.

I am convinced that the health of any church or nation depends on a sustained apprehension of the finest values of the past, and that a rootless people with no historical memory is at the mercy of any passing philosophy or transient fanaticism — "tossed to and fro," as the apostle said, "and carried about with every wind of doctrine, by the cunning of men." A nation that ignores its past is in deadly peril; and a church that tries to trim its doctrines and adjust its worship to every mood and fashion of thought has a passport to oblivion.

Having said all that, I want to raise the question at this point as to whether there is really a Protestant tradition at all. We have our heritage — the mighty impetus given to the faith by the Reformers and the vision of Christ that has lit the Protestant centuries since their times. But is there really a Protestant tradition? The Reformers themselves were conscious of only one tradition — the tradition of Christ and his apostles which they wished to rescue from everything that obscured it. They founded no church. Their one object was to reform the church that was already there. They had no desire to promulgate any doctrine that was not already in the Bible, or to invent any ceremony that could be called specifically Protestant. Luther, Calvin, and Knox professed the catholic faith, and recited the catholic creeds. They would have been horrified at the thought of our celebrating their tradition as anything different from the "faith once delivered to the saints."

Protestantism is not a tradition, but a temper of the soul. It is an alertness to the Word of God and to the needs of the time we live in. A man was called a Protestant in the sixteenth century if he responded to the Word of God, freed from the false traditions of men; and if he sought to let that Word loose with cleansing and reforming power amid the corruptions of his day. It is a tragedy that such a movement of reform had to fragment the church, and that it was canalized into denominations, each soon to develop its own fossilized traditions. Every section of the church of that time shares the blame, and the blame is still ours if we despise or neglect the summons to the visible unity of Christ's church on earth.

How many who call themselves Protestants today share the glorious freedom of the Protestant temper of soul, and how many are the slaves to a Protestant tradition? Do we congratulate ourselves that we are the heirs of a splendid tradition, rejoicing inwardly in our Protestant stock, and thanking God secretly that we are "not as other men are"? Or do we realize our deafness to the Word of God, our lack of true awareness of the world around us, and murmur: "God be merciful to me a sinner"?

The Bible is full of warnings about the dangers of dead traditions. Look at the picture of the prophet Jeremiah standing in the doorway of the Temple in Jerusalem and saying to the congregation as they came in: "Thus saith the Lord . . . trust ye not in lying words, saying, The temple of the Lord, The temple of the Lord, The temple of the Lord, are these." What an usher! Imagine if you would be met by someone at the door of your church shouting out: "Thus saith the Lord, trust ye not in lying words, saying, The Presbyterian Church, The Presbyterian Church — I'm O.K. so long as I am a member of the good old Presbyterian Church." That's how it was. This is how Jeremiah sounded the alert to a self-satisfied church.

In the time of our Lord the Pharisees were the strictest adherents to the moral and ceremonial law. They were the loyal upholders of the traditions of Israel. From contemporary reports it would appear that they were the kind of people usually regarded as the backbone of a nation, men of strict fidelity to their religious heritage. Yet what did Jesus say about their devotion to tradition? "Well did Isaiah prophesy of you hypocrites, as it is written, 'This people honors me with their lips, but their heart is far from me; in vain do they worship me, teaching as doctrines the precepts of men.' You leave the commandment of God, and hold fast the tradition of men. You have a fine way of rejecting the commandment of God, in order to keep your tradition!"

Tradition begins to have a different sound when we hear words like these. It's not that the New Testament rejects the traditions of the Old, or that Christians are summoned to live for the present hour and to reject the heritage of their fathers. The warning is that even the best tradition can be a snare, luring us into the delusion that because we have a great religious heritage we have nothing to worry about: we belong to the in-people of God.

That was the *Leitmotiv* of the preaching of John the Baptist with which the Gospels open. The Jewish people were accustomed to preachers who denounced the abominations of the heathen. They were also familiar with the practice of baptizing pagans who wanted to identify with the faith of Israel. What shook them was the appearance of this fiery prophet who reserved his denunciations for his own people, and demanded that they undergo baptism as a sign of repentance. It is hard for us to re-create the national excitement that focussed on this strip of the Jordan valley as the news of John's preaching leaked out. Crowds came from all over the land; and it was an added excitement one day when they saw a delegation of Pharisees and Sadducees in what you might call the front pews. There was the solemn tradition of Israel — the representatives of their great religious heritage, the guardians of the law and the prophets. The crowd would be wondering just how John would trim his Protestantism in the presence of these lords of the great tradition. They were in for a shock. "When he saw many of the Pharisees and Sadducees come to the baptism, he said unto them, O generation of vipers, who hath warned you to flee from the wrath to come? . . . think not to say within yourselves, We have Abraham to our father: for I say unto you, that God is able of these stones to raise up children unto Abraham."

Vipers: they knew what he meant. They had seen these little snakes squirming away from a field that was being harvested. They knew that everyone at that time was living in fear of a coming storm, and seeking some place of refuge. This was a time, like ours, of maximum insecurity. Many were looking for a place to hide, some comforting conviction that would shelter them whatever might happen. And some thought they had found their refuge. The tradition. They were Abraham's seed. God could not let anything terrible happen to those who had this wonderful heritage. John's flaming words scorched into their hopes. Tradition? Merely to be standing in a holy succession, merely to be the inheritors of a godly past, means nothing. Abraham's seed? "God is able of these stones (you can see him tossing the smooth pebbles that lie in heaps round the banks of Jordan into the air) to raise up children unto Abraham."

Do you see why I want to query the adulation of our Protestant tradition? We may imagine that the mere fact of standing in a noble line, of having good Protestant parents and ancestors, of being members of a church with roots in a rich heritage of faith and service, is enough to settle the religious question and give us a sense of inner security. The Word of God comes to us as it did to the congregation of John the Baptist. "Think not to say within yourselves, We have Luther and Calvin as our fathers; for I say unto you, that God is able of these stones to raise up children unto Luther and Calvin." We are not secured from the stones of today by virtue of being club members in a Protestant tradition. God is able of these stones — from new and unexpected places in the concrete wilderness around us — to raise up the new Protestants he needs.

Protestantism is a temper of the soul. It is the spirit of alertness to the Word of God, the living God who is active in our world today. God finds his new Protestants wherever men and women awaken to his presence and his claim. The Reformers had no new God to announce to our ancestors, but they had a new experience of his reality and power. They found that worship had become too much a mere routine, a ritual observance that had been emptied of any real sense of God's living presence and the challenge of his Word. They had one great object in the reforms they carried through — to alert the people to the reality of God, and to let them hear again his Word of judgment and of grace. They wanted to cut through the jungle of ceremony and convention to reach a real confrontation with God himself. They wanted worship to be a real participation of Christian people in an act of adoration and of dedication that they could really understand, and not to be merely passive attendants at a ritual performed on their behalf. God lives! was their message, and they sought to be a people who realized his sovereignty over every portion of their lives.

Where are God's new Protestants who stir our world with such a call today? Some might say that the new Protestants are those who are seeking to revolutionize our thoughts of God, or even to abolish them altogether. The new Protestantism is sometimes thought to be the radical secularization of our doctrines and our worship. I find little trace of the true Protestant temper of soul in a disintegrating theism that ends in Christian atheism; nor do I find it in a reform of worship that eliminates the sense of God's holy presence and commands. I find God's new Protestants wherever men and women — whatever their background or religious tradition — become alert to God's living presence, and respond in their own way to the gospel of Jesus Christ. I find God's new Protestants in these thinkers and reformers within the Roman Church today who are concerned above all with a new apprehension of the holy in our modern world, and who are carrying through a revolution of worship in which congregations become live participants, and the Word of God is seriously heard. I find God's new Protestants in those who hear the call of Christ and enter our fellowship unencumbered by the churchly traditions of the last fifty years. Such men and women bring fresh air into the conventional corridors of our worship and activities. They want reality. They want Christ — without the musty garments in which we sometimes clothe his gospel.

Protestantism is a temper of the soul. It is a spirit of alertness to the needs of the day. Mediaeval Catholicism had grown old in the service of man. We do not need to think of the pre-Reformation centuries as one long superstitious night that lay between Pentecost and Luther. It was the era of massive achievement and an often noble faith. It was the period when the cathedrals were built and the no less impressive architecture of theology developed to the glory of God. It was a time when the attempt was made to penetrate the entire life of society with the gospel of Jesus Christ. But by the sixteenth century times had changed. Corruption was widespread. New thoughts were stirring and meeting with little sympathy and understanding. It was the Protestant temper that sensed that the world was changing, that the church was bogged down in ruts of man's devising. The Protestants held firmly by the tradition of the gospel, and found that tradition come alive again through the Scriptures by the power of the Holy Spirit — the great Contemporary. But they had to reject many of the traditions that obscured the gospel and muzzled the Scriptures. They were alert to God's action in the world around them, alert to the real needs of people who in the confusions of a new age wanted desperately an unobstructed communion with their God. They were alert to the cry for freedom that came from men who were oppressed by a multitude of rules, and by clerical control. And increasingly they became alert to the cry of the oppressed, and to the silent claim of the millions around the world: "Come over and help us."

God's new Protestants are those who are helping us today to be aware of the world we live in. We may not always want to hear them: it is more comfortable to rest in our Protestant traditions. One may be telling us what is involved for the church in the explosion of scientific knowledge and technology. Another may be interpreting for us the consequences of the widening gap between the affluent and the hungry nations. Another may be trying to let us know what it feels like to live in the Harlem ghetto. Another may be alert to the surge of nationalism, or the impact of Communism, or the consequences of urbanization. We can, of course, shut our ears and tell them to go away. But the problems of a rapidly changing world will not go away. And the new Protestant is the one who is willing to face them.

Think not to say within yourselves: We have Abraham, or Paul, or Luther, or Calvin, or Knox, or Wesley, or Kierkegaard, or Schweitzer as our spiritual ancestors — unless you are willing to be as alert as they were to the presence of the living God and the needs of the times. In a church like this, at such a time as this, we cannot live on our traditions. We honor the men and women who have worshipped and served in this place, not by feeling good about them, not by doing exactly as they did in their times (not even by having their portraits painted), but by emulating their Protestant temper, learning from them how to be alert to the living God and to the needs and tempo of our times.

"God is able of these stones to raise up children unto Abraham." This is the ultimate secret of true Protestantism — the conviction that God's grace can perform the miracle of transformation, and that no one whatever is beyond the reach of the gospel of Christ. Where that gospel is proclaimed there are no outsiders. In a living church there is a tradition that can be felt, a tradition that we value; but that tradition must never become a barrier to those who feel they have not shared it. God is looking for new Protestants, and he looks both among those who have been raised in the tradition of a church like this, *and* among those whose background and experience have been totally different. He wants *you*, whoever you are, whoever your ancestors were, whatever your social or religious habits of life, and can raise *you* up to be his new Protestant in the service of Christ today.

22. *What Are the Dead Doing?*

> *And they shall see his face; and his name shall be in their foreheads. And there shall be no night there; and they need no candle, neither light of the sun; for the Lord God giveth them light; and they shall reign for ever and ever.* REVELATION 22:4-5

To many thinking people today there is something presumptuous, if not absurd, about anyone professing to know the answer to the question: What are the dead doing? How can any mortal claim to know what happens in an immortal sphere, unless on the grounds of some kind of psychic communication? Yet the Christian church has always had something to say on this subject, and has not based it on any spiritist phenomena. It is a perfectly legitimate question to ask of any minister who utters prayers, and conducts memorial services, expressing belief in resurrection and eternal life: and I believe there is a legitimate reply.

What are the dead doing? The answer to this can only be given humbly and trustfully in the form of a deduction that follows from our belief in the gospel of Jesus Christ. *Because* we believe in God; *because* we believe that Christ rose from the dead; *because* we believe in the power of the Spirit to transform these mortal lives into the image of Jesus Christ, there is something we can also believe about the nature of eternal life, and the activity of the dead. Apart from this faith in God through Christ there is nothing I can say on this subject. I have no access to the secrets of eternity of any other kind. Nothing that I have seen as evidence from spiritism or psychic research gives me any confidence in that kind of investigation. And I am not impressed with the dogmatic statements of those who claim to know all about conditions on the other side from some sectarian book or private revelation.

It is the faith we have in Jesus Christ that enables us to reach some convictions about what the dead are doing. All I have to say stems from confidence in him as the way, the truth, and life. This is how the Bible speaks about the life to come. It doesn't provide us with any precise, consistent, and detailed information about the activity of the dead. Not a single book — or even chapter — is devoted to this subject. The Old Testament practically ignores it, and the New Testament offers us what you might call flashes of insight sparked by a radiant trust in the living Christ. Far more impressive than any arguments for immortality, or than any claim to know exactly what happens in a realm beyond our sight, is the quiet assumption of Christ that such a life awaits us, and the unflinching conviction of his apostles that God has something infinitely more to give us when this mortal life is ended. "Eye hath not seen, nor ear heard, neither have entered into the heart of man, the things which God hath prepared for them that love him." That was their assurance; and it conveys both the absolute certainty that there is something for the dead to do, and the warning that our present powers of sight and hearing and contemplation are totally inadequate really to understand what this will be.

So when the Bible speaks of activity in the life beyond the grave it speaks in symbols. Whenever we are trying to convey a truth that lies beyond our normal observation — whether about the act of creation "in the beginning," or the consummation at the end of time — we must use symbols. We are learning again how vital symbols can be as instruments of highest truth. The language of music and poetry, painting and sculpture, is symbolic. So I do not hesitate to offer you as the basis for our thinking about the activity of the dead, the rich language of the New Testament book that uses symbols more than any other — the book of Revelation. Written at a time of extreme tension and danger, a time when many Christians in the prime of life were being killed, this book reflects the defiant conviction of a martyred church that there is a fullness of life beyond the grave to which God summons all who trust in him.

What kind of life is it?

"They shall see his face; and his name shall be in their foreheads." This is the first, and ultimately all-sufficient answer to our question. The activity of the dead is *adoration.* The chief end of man, both now and in the hereafter, is "to glorify God and to enjoy him for ever." Here we find the Christian answer to the question about what our ultimate goal is meant to be; it is the vision of God. Since we today are not soaked in and surrounded by the thought of God as the one with whom we have to do, perhaps it is hard for us to get the full force of this statement: "They shall see his face." In an era when God tends to be either a familiar, friendly figure in the background, or else just an abstract idea of ultimate power and meaning, "vision of God" is not a compelling or exciting theme. But if we begin to recapture the biblical Word of a Lord of transcendent glory and devastating purity, if we have any glimpse of what is implied by the words: "Holy, holy, holy, Lord God of hosts; Heaven and earth are full of thy glory. Glory be to thee, O Lord Most High"; then we may understand a little better this activity of adoration when "they shall see his face." For the first Christians who were reared on the Old Testament it was an axiom that no mortal man could gaze on the face of God. Do you remember the word of Moses? "Thou canst not see my face; for there shall no man see me and live." In symbolic language we are told that even the glimpse of God "from behind" that was given to Moses was of such overwhelming glory that when he returned to his people he carried such a reflection of it that he had to veil his countenance. Yet here it is boldly said that the dead in Christ "shall see his face." Whatever else is meant we are surely to understand that in the life to come the highest activity conceivable is the adoration of God in a dimension of inconceivable nearness and unclouded vision.

Is this kind of activity beyond the understanding of people like us who live in a very different world from that of Moses or the writer of the Revelation? Only if we attempt to unravel the symbols and read poetry as prose. Otherwise we are just as able as any other generation to realize that adoration can be the highest activity of man. Think of the moments you have known of purest rapture, when time stood still and you seemed to touch a new level of existence. Think of the times, few and fleeting though they may have been, when you had a holy awareness, an indescribable sense of beauty, love, and peace. Think of the occasional high point you have known in worship, when a word opened a new door in the soul, when grace came unexpectedly with the bread and wine of Holy Communion. You would not trade such moments for the best a merely secular world can offer. And yet they are but a dim reflection of the activity of adoration that is open to the dead.

"And his name shall be in their foreheads." Again, the symbol — the symbol of an absolute belonging. We cannot hide from ourselves the fact that the activity of adoration has meaning only for those who are, consciously or unconsciously, yielded to the living God. The mere fact of physical death does not, as it were, automatically qualify everybody for this glorious vision of God. I make no claim to know how any may exclude himself from this vision, how he may be enabled to grow gradually towards it, or what his education in adoration may turn out to be. I only know that this is said of those who confess they belong to God, and who are learning to worship him here and now: "They shall see his face." As another apostle put it, "Beloved, now are we the sons of God, and it doth not yet appear what we shall be: but we know that, when he shall appear, we shall be like him; for we shall see him as he is."

If adoration — an adoration more absorbing and satisfying and active than we can now begin to guess — is the chief occupation of heaven, what else may we reasonably believe? "There shall be no night there; and they need no candle, neither light of the sun; for the Lord God giveth them light; and they shall reign for ever and ever."

The night with its candles — surely the symbol of the restless quest of man for knowledge, for understanding of his mysterious existence, for some light on the nature of the universe in which he is so precariously poised on this tiny planet. If adoration is an activity of which we have some fragmentary experience, surely *exploration* is one of which in this generation we know much more. The candles of science and philosophy are lit across the countries and around the world. Man will not accept the darkness. In every age it is a cavern to be explored, a dark womb from which new knowledge may be brought to birth. What are they doing, these endless generations of men and women who stretch through history from the time that a creature appeared who could be called man? What distinguished them from their cousins in the animal world is surely this: they have been continually busy lighting candles, sending little shafts of light into the obscurities of their strange surroundings. Man is an explorer, and every one of us, so long as there is spirit within him, continues to light candles in the dark.

And what are the dead doing? "They need no candle, neither light of the sun." Does this mean that their quest is ended, that now they rest in endless light, like sunbathers on some everlasting beach? I believe the opposite. "The Lord God giveth them light: and they shall reign for ever and ever." Does that sound like passivity? Like the "saints' everlasting rest"?

The contrast between our candles in the night and the light that streams unbroken from the throne of God does indeed suggest that the exploration of the dead is different from ours. As St. Paul put it: "Now we see through a glass darkly: but then face to face: now I know in part: but then shall I know even as also I am known." The conditions of knowledge will obviously be totally different in the eternal dimension. Even in this world we know the difference between exploration in the dark and exploration in the light. When a man falls in love he is often, as it were, groping in the dark; but if happy marriage comes he begins what you might call an exploration in the light. In medical research there is a long period of exploration in the dark, but with a new discovery there comes a time of further exploration in the light. So we may begin to guess at what is meant by, "The Lord God giveth them light: and they shall reign for ever and ever."

What are the dead doing? Surely they are exploring in

the new dimension of eternal light. I think I know something of what is meant by "the rest that remaineth for the people of God," the hope expressed in Shakespeare's words, "After life's fitful fever he sleeps well." There is a sense in which heaven must reflect that "the strife is o'er, the battle done." But I find nothing in the Scriptures to encourage the idea that heaven is a dull plateau of idleness, where billions of the dead do nothing for ever and ever to the eternal muzak of the harp. "He also that had received two talents came and said, Lord, thou deliveredst unto me two talents: behold, I have gained two other talents beside them. His lord said unto him, Well done, good and faithful servant: thou hast been faithful over a few things"—I will pension you off? No: "I will make thee ruler over many things: enter thou into the joy of thy lord." If the entering into the joy of the Lord can stand for adoration, this being made ruler over many things surely stands for the exploration and the still greater responsibility that await us. Every reference in the New Testament suggests that the dead are not idle. This is the summons to action that sounds in the symbol of dominion: "They shall reign for ever and ever." It is an echo of the creative word: "Let us make man in our image, after our likeness, and let them have dominion."

The exploration in the light, and the new authority conferred, are the foundation of my belief that there is work to be done beyond the grave. Only thus can I understand why some of the best we have known have been taken from this world, often at the height of their powers. They have gone to the sphere of adoration where "they shall see his face"; and they have also gone to a world of light where there is a new dimension for exploration and the exercise of their God-given gifts.

A service of worship is not only an opportunity to reflect on these things and to renew our faith. In a very real sense it is an anticipation of the world to come. For here we learn to adore. Here we have those glimpses of eternity when we know that there is nothing more ultimate and satisfying than the vision of God. Here the material world, with its bread and wine, can be the vehicle of our union with the eternal world where Christ is King. And here we can begin that exploration into light that is the joyful activity of the company of heaven. What the dead are doing we can begin to do. This is part of what we mean when we say: "I believe in the communion of saints."

23. *Church of the Real or Museum of the Trivial?*

The kingdom we are given is unshakable; let us therefore give thanks to God, and so worship him as he would be worshipped, with reverence and awe; for our God is a devouring fire. HEBREWS 12:28-29 (NEB)

Dr. Tom Driver once said that "the church can have many sins and still live: but the sin that kills it is the sin of preferring the unreal to the real." I believe that he is perfectly right: this disease is a killer. And what makes it doubly dangerous is that we usually don't know when we are suffering from it. It is possible to live with the unreal so long that it literally becomes our religion. Then inside a church we can indulge in a kind of fantasy life: we meet the real world again when we emerge on the street. Worse still, we may carry out from the sanctuary to the avenue a preference for the unreal that it so abundantly provides.

Such a challenge drives me back to the Bible. For, as I have often pointed out from this pulpit, the Bible is the most realistic of books. It contains no flighty philosophy, no woolly idealism, no bogus sentiment, no comforting statistics, and no ghostly platitudes. It is a book of real people, real events, real love, real hates, real life, real death, and a real God. And when it speaks of worship it does not offer a picture of pretty pieties and relaxing slogans.

There is nothing vague and nothing soothing about the words of our text: "The kingdom we are given is unshakable; let us therefore give thanks to God, and so worship him as he would be worshipped, with reverence and awe; for our God is a devouring fire." The same note rings through the familiar words of the Fourth Gospel: "God is a spirit, and those who worship him must worship in spirit and truth." "Spirit and truth." Truth here *means* reality. In our use of the words "spiritual" and "spirituality" we often imply the very opposite: they refer to something vaguely cozy and totally unreal. "Spirit and reality" — what God hath joined together let no man put asunder.

I believe therefore that as a church becomes more alert to the Spirit of God it will be more and more a church of the real. That means a more real worship where we give thanks to a real God, "and so worship him as he would be worshipped, with reverence and awe." Unreal worship occurs when we simply go through familiar motions and settle back to be soothed, to be mentally entertained, or to have our prejudices confirmed. A church of the real will be concerned with real people, not cards on an index; with the real problems and agonies of our day, and not with trivialities; with real encounters where men and women expose their real beliefs, and not merely the surface politenesses behind which the real self is hidden. There has probably never been a church at any time that was completely real. There is always a measure of unreality when people group themselves together for any purpose whatever. But of all such human groupings the church of Jesus Christ should be by far the most real. And the question we have to ask is simply this: are we, in relation to the world that we live in, becoming more, or less, real in our worship, our fellowship, our concerns, our activities?

This is probably the most searching and urgent question to be asked of any church at the present hour. For when I talk with those who are outside the church, or read what some of them write, I have the impression that what holds back many alert and intelligent men and women of goodwill from any commitment to, or even interest in, the church's cause today is a sense of unreality. Rightly or wrongly, they have come to associate the church's worship and activity in the modern world with religious nostalgia — a nostalgia they are willing to share on the limited basis of Christmas and Easter, with pretense, with bogus beliefs, with unreality and triviality. We may sing: "Like a mighty army moves the church of God," but the image in many minds today is rather of a museum where certain ancestral religious traditions are preserved. But perhaps even the word "museum" is now misleading, for we are surrounded by museums that are alive and alert to the real world we live in. The tragedy is that many have come to think of the church as a museum of the trivial; that the things we are preserving are irrelevant, and the matters that excite us are of no real importance.

In giving this picture of the churches as seen by many who are outside I am not scoring points off any section of the church, or indulging in the cheap pastime of caricaturing the institution I am ordained to serve. I am simply trying to be realistic. And it is unreal to imagine that the churches in our modern cities are generally seen to be dynamic communities of blazing faith and vigorous involvement in the real questions of the day. We are rushing into a future of unimaginable change and extraordinary potential for good or evil. Does the average man really see the churches as a real factor in that future? Let me give you one example of what people think. At the New York World's Fair it was possible to take a tour through the city of the future. There it was in all its mechanical splendor and technological glory, a vision of how we, or our children, may be living fifty, or even twenty, years from now. Everything gleamed and glittered with the achievements of a generation that is conquering the elements and eliminating the maladies of the past. And the church? There it was — a little corner of spirituality, a Gothic huddle completely unrelated to the new world, a museum of religion in a city that was complete without it.

If we are to be realistic we must listen also to the voice of the younger generation. Never has the pressure been so great from the swelling numbers of the under twenty-fives, and never perhaps has there been so wide a gulf between their thinking and that of the older generation. It is not enough to sigh over their explosions of rebellion, or smugly to remark that in the end they'll settle down and be like us. They don't want to be like us — either in our social life, our political life, or our religious life. And the criticism they bring to bear on all of these centers is this problem of unreality and pretense. Whatever their faults this "take-over generation," as it has been called, is violently allergic to sham and the bogus, and hungry for reality wherever it can be found. It is my impression that they are by no means antagonistic to religion, but find themselves repelled by all that appears to them trivial, fake, and totally unreal in the words and works of the churches. Where they sense reality in religion, where, to at least some extent, their language is spoken, where real issues are discussed, where real contact is made with the world of today, and where the gospel of Christ is seen to make a real difference in the way people behave, you will find that this new generation is responding more eagerly than my own. One of the most frequent questions asked me by students in high school and college goes like this: "Is there really any difference between the way church members and non-church members think and act in everyday life?" They are shrewd enough to know that a religion that has no practical consequences is unreal.

How, then, do we move towards the real? How can we, as individual Christians and as a church, avoid this sin of preferring the unreal to the real? How can we become that church of God's design, that point in the modern world where we are nearer to the real than anywhere else, that community where there is less sham and more honesty, less superficiality and more depth, less triviality and more reality, than in any other group we know?

Reality must begin with our worship, with our personal and congregational communion with God. If there is no reality in this everything else is bound to dissolve in triviality and sham. Unreality can begin at the very idea of prayer and worship. If we don't think that what we are doing is really important, if the kingdom of God is just a vague notion at the back of our minds, something that ebbs and flows according to the mood of the moment, if worship is just a routine in which we were raised, and if God himself is really a minor factor in our thinking, a kind of side bet in case other measures should fail, then the unreal has taken over, and the church is already for us a museum of the trivial. Reality begins when we have at least some idea of what these words mean: "The kingdom we are given is unshakable; let us therefore give thanks to God, and so worship him as he would be worshipped, with reverence and awe; for our God is a devouring fire."

"An unshakable kingdom . . . God . . . a devouring fire." That's reality — and a reality that we have often obscured by shunting this whole area of belief into the "may be" section of our minds. We prefer to keep the thought of God at a comfortable distance, and his kingdom "out there" in some spiritual fairyland. There's a sting in the tail of this text which we must have noticed. Wouldn't we expect the writer to say something like this: "let us give thanks to God, and so worship him as he would be worshipped, with reverence and awe; for our God is a loving Father"? That would be perfectly true, but this time the Word is different. "Our God is a devouring fire." Do we quietly excise this phrase as a remnant of a more primitive religion? Then we must be prepared to expurgate the entire New Testament, for it is not only in the oldest strata of the Old Testament that this figure is used. Who was it who came to "baptize with the Holy Ghost and with fire"? Who was it who said: "I am come to send fire on the earth"? Fire is a symbol of cleansing, of the burning away of all impurity. The God who is a devouring fire is not some monster seeking to devour his creatures. He is the God who is so real, so near, so holy, and so good, that in his presence all unreality is consumed like dry leaves in a furnace.

What we are being told is that true worship begins with the realization that we are seeking a real God who must be approached with reverence and awe. As we bow in *his* presence the fire has already begun to devour the trivialities and unrealities of our surface life so that the real person is exposed before him. I do not therefore believe that we reach towards reality by abandoning the Bible picture of a God who is, in some sense of the word, personal. It is because he is one who speaks to us, and to whom we can speak, one who is the most real person in the universe; that in his presence we strip away the unreality and begin to know who we really are. Reality is not found by purging away all that the Bible says about a living, active God who is not only creator of all things visible and invisible, but has to do with each individual human being, substituting some abstract concept acceptable to that other abstraction called "the modern mind." The God we come here to worship, the God we seek to serve in daily life, is more real than the rocket leaping into space, more real than the man next door. That is the amazing testimony of the Bible, and of the company of all the saints. So real is he, according to the good news of the New Testament, that "when the fulness of the time was come," his Word, his revelation of himself, his communication with us, "was made flesh, and dwelt among us."

Reality begins with this encounter with the living God, and real worship demands that we stop to remember this. What I have said by no means implies that no one should come to church who is not utterly convinced that God is real, and that he has revealed himself to us in Jesus Christ. Real worship means the searching as well as the finding. We are not divided into those who have an intense belief in the reality of God and those who have not. We are all, I hope, in search of this reality, at varying stages of conviction. There can be more reality about the prayer: "Lord, I am utterly confused, but I want to know" or "Lord, I believe, help thou mine unbelief," than in the passive acceptance of prayers we do not really share, the singing of hymns we do not really mean, or the recital of creeds we have not bothered to examine.

Worship becomes more real as we learn to take part. That is the real point in responses, and prayers said together. That is the reason for sacraments in which a whole congregation is involved. And what is more real than the sacraments themselves? It is as if God were saying: "Just in case my message to you should get lost in words, just in case you miss the gospel in the verbiage of the preacher, I'm giving you this water to use in baptism, this bread and wine to use in Holy Communion." Unreality has been reinforced by the neglect of the sacraments in our tradition, by the infrequency of Communion, and the edging of baptism out of the communal worship of the church. Mysteries? Yes: but mysteries that are the gateway to the real.

As I am sharing with you in this search for the real in our church's life, let me confess that I am aware that the preacher too — perhaps more than any — can contribute to the unreal, the phony, and the trivial. Just recently I heard a story that had in it for me something of that devouring fire. In the frontier days there was a village out west whose people were engaged in the lumbering trade. They built a church and called a minister. He went out to them and was well received. In fact they became very fond of him, and he of them. He conducted the services, visited their homes, and the church prospered. Then one day as he was by the riverside he happened to see some of his parishioners clawing into the bank some logs that had been floating down from another village higher up the river. They were marked with the owner's stamp on the end of each log. To his great distress he saw that his parishioners were pulling in the logs and sawing off a little piece at the end where the tell-tale stamp appeared. Next Sunday he had prepared a mighty sermon. The text was "Thou shalt not steal" and it was delivered with great fervor and powerful exposition. At the close of the service his congregation lined up and congratulated him with enthusiasm. "Wonderful sermon," they said, "mighty fine preaching!" This naturally troubled him quite a lot, so he went home and worked at a sermon for the following Sunday. This time he announced his text: "Thou shalt not cut off the end of thy neighbors' logs." When he had got through they ran him out of town.

Yes: reality means more than being conscious of the presence of the living God in worship. It means more than being aware that his Word is being truly preached. It means that worship must reshape the way we live, the decisions we take, the part we play in the life of our community. It means experiencing the Word as, in this same writer's words, "alive and active. It cuts more keenly than any two-edged sword, piercing as far as the place where life and spirit, joints and marrow divide. It sifts the purposes and thoughts of the heart."

For the prophet Isaiah much of the worship of his day was totally unreal. The Temple was becoming a museum of triviality. To him the Word of God came as a devouring fire. "To what purpose is the multitude of your sacrifices unto me? . . . I am full of the burnt offerings of rams, and the fat of fed beasts . . . bring no more vain oblations . . . your new moons and your appointed feasts my soul hateth; they are a trouble to me; I am weary to bear them . . . . Wash you, make you clean; . . . cease to do evil, learn to do well; seek judgment, relieve the oppressed, judge the fatherless, plead for the widow." Then — and only then — do the words appear: "Come now, let us reason together, saith the Lord."

But even this we can hear as a famous passage of Scripture too distant to be real. Suppose we translate: "What do your church services really mean? I'm tired of prayers that imply no action, of hymns that just warm the emotions, of sermons that change nothing in your way of life. Wash you, make you clean. Be really honest with your family, in your work, in your business. Support those who are working for racial justice, for the abolition of poverty, for protecting the rights of the weak, for feeding the hungry. Take your part in efforts to clean up the city. Stop repeating the gossip and slogans that feed prejudice and hate."

My confidence that the churches can meet the future, that they will not lapse into mere museums of triviality, lies in the constant power of renewal by the Spirit of God. Even the religious institution flayed by the prophet Isaiah not only endured to be a living force right to the present day, but became the cradle in which the Christian church was born. And it was from among men and women entangled in the superficialities and trivialities of a petty legalism that Jesus Christ found the apostles of his future church. Time and again that church has seemed to be foundering in the quicksands of triviality, and then has heard the Word of renewal. "Our God is a devouring fire" — and he stands ready to scorch away the unreal and the trivial from our church's life today.

Let us ask ourselves as we seek to be alert for these years ahead: "What is real, and what is unreal, in our worship, our prayers, our meetings, and our fellowship, our activities, our share in the mission of the church?" Much that is just words is unreal. Some things that take up our time are trivial. Unreality from the world outside in the form of sentimentality, shoddy thinking, bad art, bogus beliefs, seeps into the church. But when we touch here the presence of the living God — that is reality. When we meet the crucified and risen Christ — that is reality. When the Bible talks straight to our condition — that is reality. When a defeated man or woman finds new hope, a lonely soul real friendship, a confused child a light to live by, a student a new meaning for existence, the battered and the bruised a helping hand — there is reality. A couple sincerely exchanging Christian vows of marriage, a child offered to God in Holy Baptism, a Christian funeral confessing our faith in the life eternal — there is reality. God give us grace to prefer, to seek, and to proclaim the real.

24. *"Christ Came"*

I came from the Father and have come into the world. Now I am leaving the world again and going to the Father. His disciples said, "Why, this is plain speaking; this is no figure of speech." JOHN 16:28-9 (NEB)

Plain speaking? No figure of speech? This is where we part company with the disciples. The words may be simple enough but their meaning is by no means plain to us today. And the word "Father," applied to God, is most certainly a figure of speech; and so is the expression "I came." Some of us may hear words like these so often that we do accept them as plain and straightforward, but there are millions for whom they are so metaphorical as to be practically meaningless. The difficulty is not in the words themselves — they are all very simple — but in the picture they conjure up in our minds. If you had never heard of Jesus Christ, but read one day that a certain man who had made a deep impression by his life and teaching had made this remark: "I came from the Father and have come into the world," just what would you make of it? Came? Then where was he before? And who is this Father? If he means God then is God somewhere else so that there was some kind of journey to be made? And who else in the long story of the world's great men has ever talked like this about his origin and birth?

I raise these questions, not just as a kind of word-game for the interest of the few who have a mind for metaphysics, or make a hobby of semantics. There are easier things to preach about in the Advent season. I want to reach through with you to the very center of this Advent message, because it has to do with what we believe about Jesus Christ. And what we believe about Jesus Christ is going in the end to affect everything we do. If the Bible is saying something about the origin of Christ that we cannot understand in today's language, then this is serious for us all. If the traditional teaching of the church about the coming of Christ is not acceptable any longer we shall have to face the consequences. And if, in fact, we have been quite unconscious of any difficulty in these familiar phrases, might it not be because we have never brought the language we use in church into contact with the language of the world outside?

"I came from the Father and have come into the world." Whatever these words may mean they clearly imply a unique claim. The solemn emphasis here, and elsewhere in the New Testament, on Christ's "coming" from the Father, shows us that these words are not to be taken in the sense of the popular religious saying that "we all come from God and we all go to God." (Even that remark is not all that obvious to the average man today.) What the men who wrote the New Testament have announced to the world is the conviction that this Christ, whose life and death they record, had a unique origin; that his birth marked a unique link between this world we know and another world that is divine and eternal, and therefore a new point of departure for the human race; and that it is his divine origin and destiny that enables him to be the Savior of the world. If we can wrestle through to an understanding of these strange words: "Christ *came*" in the light both of the Bible and the kind of universe science reveals to us today, then we shall be more alert and equipped Christians for the tasks at hand, and Advent and Christmas will regain the meaning they have been tending to lose.

From the questions people ask me about the orthodox doctrines concerning Christ, about his incarnation, his divinity, his miracles, the virgin birth, the resurrection, and the words in the Creed about his "coming to judge the quick and the dead," I get the impression that many have wrapped all these matters up in a little cobwebby box marked: "Top Sacred," and are not quite sure where to put it. Inside the church there is a tendency to believe that the clergy, the officers, and good church members have all accepted the complete package while I am the one with doubts. Hence what I have called the "conspiracy of silence" about sharing our real beliefs and real disbeliefs. There is an idea abroad that once the box is opened we'll find that so many doctrines will wither away in the light of our modern thinking that little, if anything, will be left. So much publicity is given to those who pry open the box publicly and announce their disbeliefs that we are inclined to forget that it is very possible to have our faith immensely strengthened by the process of investigation.

Suppose we raise boldly this vital question of the origins of Christ. Where did he come from? What was his background? How do we estimate the forces that shaped his character, influenced his thought and expression, and led to that meteoric ministry, cut short by execution at an early age? We do not worship a ghost in the Christian church, but a real person. Those who refuse to ask such questions may think that they are conserving a sacred heritage and protecting it from violation by impious hands, but in fact they are falling into one of the most series heresies of all. In the early days of the church it was called Docetism — and Docetism meant that Jesus Christ only *appeared* to be real man but was really a vision of God flashing into the world of men like a kind of heavenly spectre. When our oldest creeds were composed the church was more worried about people who denied the humanity of Christ than those who denied his divinity. And there are many rugged defenders of what they think is orthodoxy today who leave our Lord on such a pedestal of unapproachable divinity that he ceases to be real.

We begin then our questions about his origin quite rightly on the human level. This is what the first three Gospels do. St. Mark introduces Jesus as a young man who experiences a divine call to action during a mission conducted by John the Baptist on the banks of the Jordan River. If we read this account and what follows with fresh eyes, removing any dogmatic spectacles we are accustomed to wear, we shall find one answer to the question: Where did Christ come from? He came from a specific Jewish milieu at a time of great national tension. It becomes obvious that we can't begin to understand many of the things he said and did unless we take account of the strong currents that were running at that time and the religious and political situation of the day. The origins of Jesus are bound up with his Jewish heritage and specific expectations of the time. He came from a people who had had a unique experience among the nations of the Middle East, and his words and actions were clearly influenced by his legacy of frustration and of hope. Therefore we shall soon discover that much of the account of his life and death is unintelligible without some understanding of the writings of the Old Testament — supplemented by the increasingly available material that comes from more contemporary sources, the kind of writings represented by the Dead Sea Scrolls.

Many of you will have read or (our favorite substitute for reading books) seen reviews of the book by Hugh Schonfield called *The Passover Plot.* When we realize that this "Plot" is revealed to be a deliberate plan of Jesus to fake death on the cross in order to fulfill messianic prophecies by coming alive again, we may be shocked, stunned, or wildly indignant. But this is not a book to be despised, or to be afraid of. Its climax will not, I think, convince many independent scholars, let alone those who are Christian believers. But the description of the origins of Jesus in the preceding chapters, and of the forces at work in the Palestine of his time, is brilliant and illuminating. We are shown the immense importance that was attached to the word "Messiah," and the intense conviction of Jesus that God had chosen him to be that deliverer of his people. Schonfield shows him as a masterful, courageous, sincere, and utterly dedicated Jew, prepared to go through to the bitter end in fulfillment of the destiny he had assumed.

So this is one answer. Jesus came from this background and when we know something of what was pulsing in that corner of the Roman world, we have the clue to his character. It is, however, very evident that Schonfield has to treat the records in a certain way. Not all, for instance, that St. Mark reports about Jesus fits this theory

— and no other. So he falls back on the usual device of excising those passages that show a Jesus who is not altogether to be understood in this historical framework. Anything that hints at a unique supernatural power, any claim that goes beyond that of the expected Messiah, any incident that involves a truly divine intervention, is written off as pious additions to the story by the early Christians.

But suppose we keep an open mind. Already in St. Mark's Gospel — and very early in the story — we find hints that the origins of this Jesus are not only to be found in contemporary Judaism. This man not only heals the bodies and minds of men, he forgives sins — a divine prerogative. And he speaks of his own origins in terms that are not mere references to his human heritage. It is in St. Mark's Gospel that we find his words: "The Son of man came not to be ministered unto, but to minister, and to give his life a ransom for many." Here it is — that little word "came." That's not how men — even the greatest religious or political leaders — speak of their origins.

If we follow up this hint and turn to St. Matthew and St. Luke, we find a very remarkable introduction to the story of Jesus. They take his origins farther back. While St. Mark starts with his call at the River Jordan, they set out the story of his birth. In one sense it is a very normal, human story; and again the emphasis is on the spiritual heritage of this child. The narrative coruscates with quotations from the Old Testament, and the songs of Elizabeth and of Mary are pure Hebrew psalms. But there is something else. The authors are telling us that this was, after all, no ordinary birth. However you interpret the stories of the shepherds and the angels and the wise men, and whether or not you accept the statement that Jesus had no human father, you cannot miss the note of wonder, the conviction that this simple birth to a peasant girl has cosmic significance, that this was an event that uniquely linked this mortal world with the immortal and invisible realm of God. This is not sheer embellishment of an otherwise drab story, nor is it crude miracle-mongering in the interests of later doctrine. It is a witness to the conviction of the first Christians that in a unique sense *Christ came* — he was not simply born like the rest of us. In this Child was the presence of the living and eternal God. That is the astounding claim behind such music as the words of annunciation: "The Holy Ghost shall come upon thee, and the power of the Highest shall overshadow thee: therefore also that holy thing that shall be born of thee shall be called the Son of God."

Now we are ready to open the last of the Gospels and see how in the end it was possible to speak of the origins of Christ. When this writer had pondered what St. Mark had to say about the call of Jesus at his baptism, and what St. Matthew and St. Luke had to say about his human birth, his mind travelled back through time and eternity to find words to express what they now had all begun to see in this Christ with whom they had lived and talked. And with the audacity of faith he dares to echo the opening words of the book of Genesis. "In the beginning," he writes, "was the Word, and the Word was with God, and the Word was God." The words of the prologue roll on. He is going to have much to tell us about this Jesus who lived, and talked, and ate and drank, and suffered and died, but before all else he wants to tell us where he came from, and who he truly is. "In him was life; and the life was the light of men." "And the Word was made flesh, and dwelt among us, and we beheld his glory, the glory as of the only begotten of the Father, full of grace and truth."

Christ came. The Word — the revelation, the out-going of God in creation from all eternity, the expression of his being — this Word became flesh. Just what does it mean for us today? "Coming" is, of course, a figure of speech — even though the disciples didn't think so. At any rate it certainly does not mean that there was a location somewhere in outer space where God lives, and from which he literally sent his Son to earth at so many miles per hour. And, in spite of the constant caricaturing of some modern writers, I doubt if any intelligent Christian really ever thought like this. I believe that neither the Bible writers, nor the so-called man-in-the-pew, are quite so dumb as our radical theologians would like to think. If you are talking about communication between the divine world of the ultimate and eternal and this earth we know, and if such communication is not just "Word" but "Word made flesh," what other metaphor can you use than that of coming? If to the statement "Christ came" you want to reply, "From where?" the answer must be, "From the environment of God, the total environment, that dimension that includes and transcends the universe we know."

This is the one point at which we may decide whether for us this Advent word of "coming" can make any sense. If there is no other sphere of existence than this world we see, and touch, and measure; if there is no dimension, whether expressed in terms of depth or height, than that of our secular experience; if there is no presence of God that is infinitely more near and real than anything we have experienced in space and time, then clearly it means nothing to talk of Christ's coming. We shall have to find his origins and significance entirely within the plane of our secular history. But if we are not enslaved by this secularist fundamentalism, and have minds and spirits open to the reality of the transcendent world, if the word "God" still conveys to us something much more than the sum total of all we are able to observe or the best that man has been, then we may hear again the words of the one whose earthly origins we know when he tells us whence he comes and whither he goes. "I came from the Father and have come into the world. Now I am leaving the world again and going to the Father."

The world — and somewhere else. There is no way of removing this contrast from the gospel. You cannot secularize the Christian faith without rewriting the New Testament. The world — and that which is not the world, that which includes it, penetrates it, transcends it. We may listen to the poet talking:

> *Of something far more deeply interfused,*
> *Whose dwelling is the light of setting suns,*
> *And the round ocean and the living air,*
> *And the blue sky, and in the mind of man.*

Or we may listen to the scientist:

> My religion [said Albert Einstein] consists of a humble admiration of the illimitable superior spirit who reveals himself in the slight details we are able to

> perceive with our frail and feeble minds. That deeply emotional conviction of the presence of a superior reasoning power, which is revealed in the incomprehensible universe, forms my idea of God.

Or we may listen to the prophet:

> Have ye not known? Have ye not heard? . . . it is he that sitteth on the circle of the earth, and the inhabitants thereof are as grasshoppers; that stretcheth out the heavens as a curtain, and spreadeth them out as a tent to dwell in.

Or we may listen to the apostle:

> We look not at the things which are seen, but the things that are not seen: for the things which are seen are temporal; but the things which are not seen are eternal.

Call it transcendent, supernatural, the ultimate reality, what you will — it is from this most real presence that Jesus came and to which he returned. He is the one who, in his secular life here on earth, in his demonstration of love in action and passion, has linked these two worlds together. When we say "Christ came," we may be using a figure of speech — but what a figure, and what speech! For how does he describe this world invisible, this ultimate reality? "I came from the mystery"? "I came from the dark background of existence"? "I came from the world of power, infinite and uncontrolled"? No: "I came from the Father." This is the word he used to tell us what the ultimate really is, what the final truth looks like. Father. And what kind of a Father? *His* Father, the one whose nature he perfectly reflects: When we celebrate Advent and Christmas, when we talk about the coming of Christ, when we talk about his divinity, we are not spinning dogmas to confuse the mind. We are simply responding to the greatest news that ever broke upon this world — that the heart of all things, the final mystery, the world of ultimate meaning, God himself, is made known to us in the kind of life, the kind of death, and the kind of love that we know in Jesus Christ. To use another figure of speech, he has told us "there are many mansions." Then he added: "I go to prepare a place for you." This is not just promise for the future.

By God's grace we find that place now — the place where this mortal life is touched by the world eternal, and where the secular is lit by the holy.

25. *Mammon — Master or Servant?*

Ye cannot serve God and mammon.
MATTHEW 6:24

Mammon.

I found recently, by conducting an informal poll, that while most people are vaguely familiar with this text, hardly anyone knew what Mammon was. I imagine that if it were suddenly to appear on the billboards, on the side of buses, or in whole-page advertisements without explanation, some would think it the title of a new musical, others a breakfast food or a deodorant. If it appeared as the title of a lecture many would think it the name of some strange new god. Others might begin to remember something from the Bible and place Mammon among the deities that were off-limits to the Israelites in the Old Testament — Baal, Dagon, Ashtoreth, Moloch, Chemosh, and the rest. It's the kind of word you come across in a crossword puzzle. You've heard it somewhere but you're not sure exactly what it means.

Yet there's no real mystery about it. The plain truth is that, in the language that Jesus spoke, Mammon was the word for money. Why the Aramaic word was retained when the Greek New Testament was written no one really knows. Apparently one or two other Aramaic words were so frequently used by Jesus that they were retained when the Greek Gospels were written. "Abba," meaning "Father," is one of them. We can well understand that the special emphasis that he put upon this word could lead to it being adopted in another tongue, but it rather surprises us to learn that he talked so often about money that his own word for this too passed into other languages. Yet so it was. Mammon was the everyday word in the Aramaic he normally spoke for "money." You will find that in our text the New English Bible has cut the corners and simply translates: "You cannot serve God and Money."

If, in the back of your mind, there is still an idea hovering around that Mammon is some kind of a god it came, not from the Bible, but like many other popular pictures, from John Milton, the poet. In the beginning of "Paradise Lost" Milton portrays the Devil and his minions as angels in heaven who revolt against God and are

Hurled headlong flaming from th' ethereal sky
With hideous ruin and combustion down
To bottomless perdition.

Among these fallen angels he lists some of the pagan deities from the Old Testament, and then creates a new one — Mammon. He knew perfectly well what he was doing, for the very words of our text "You cannot serve God and Mammon" suggest that here is a rival deity. And the picture Milton gives of Mammon as one of the leaders in the revolt against the Almighty shows us the allure of material wealth competing with the vision of God.

Mammon led them on,
Mammon, the least erected Spirit that fell
From heaven, for even in heaven his looks and thoughts
Were always downward bent, admiring more
The riches of heaven's pavement, trodden gold,
Than aught divine or holy else enjoyed
In vision beatific.

Whenever later writers wanted to speak of money in its alluring and demonic power, money as a god that is worshipped, money as a tyrant among men, they often have used the word Mammon. But on Jesus' lips it simply meant money, money as the sign and symbol of our material possessions.

When it first dawned on me that our Lord had so much to say about money, I wondered why. It was not that I was surprised to discover in the Bible an emphasis on something so material and everyday. That's the kind of book it is — dealing with the hard facts and practicalities of daily life far more than with abstract ideas. I just wondered why he should refer so often to this one aspect of our material life — money, possessions, property. Then I noticed that the references are not all of a kind. He warns against the misuse of money, against the worship of money, against reliance on money; but he also speaks of the positive use of money, its employment as an agent of love (as when the Good Samaritan arranged to pay the hotel bill for the wounded traveller), its investment (as in the parable of the talents), even of its extraction for the payment of taxes. He doesn't list money among the good things we are to seek, but neither does he include it among the evils we are to shun. It is the great neutral, waiting to be enlisted for good or evil ends.

I began to see that money in his eyes is a huge potential in the hands of man, like atomic power in our day, to be used for constructive or destructive ends. And it is power that is, to a greater or less degree, put into the hands of every one of us. Our money is an intimate part of us. It represents the extension of our personality in all kinds of surprising ways within the human family. What we do with our money reflects very accurately the kind of people we are. Just because it is *ours,* our property, our possession, it becomes the crucial point in the exercise of our God-given freedom. Since Jesus Christ was concerned above all else with our right use of this freedom, with our choosing the kingdom of God, with our choosing the narrow and not the easy way, with our choosing to return to the Father rather than to stay in the far country, with our choosing to follow him rather than our own devices, he saw the enormous importance of money as the crucial test of our decision. In the ultimate choice between a life devoted to God and life devoted to self, he knew that our attitude to money is decisive, for money is the self made visible. Hence instead of saying: You can't worship God *and* worship yourself; you can't at the same time make God the center of your life *and* yourself," he simply said: "You cannot serve God *and* money."

"No man can serve two masters." Our Lord knows

how prone we are to make the attempt. There are very few who deliberately make money their God and renounce all allegiance to the Father in heaven. But in practice how many of us can say that we have never experienced a divided loyalty? Just how many of our decisions are dictated by Mammon and how many by God? Have we never known moments when, even in a small way, there has been a battle between our conscience and an opportunity for financial gain? Who gives the orders — that's the point — God or Mammon? When we hear a text like this we are quick to get out from under by letting it refer to some mythical monster who literally makes money his god. We think of a Shylock counting his ducats, of a ruthless tycoon who cares for nothing and nobody except the growth of his fortune, of the miser who revels in the very feel of his wealth, the slave of Mammon worshipping his golden calf. But there were not many millionaires among the congregation who heard the Sermon on the Mount, and Jesus was certainly not aiming at some absent target. He knew that every single one of us, from the moment we snatch at a toy in the nursery and yell, "It's *mine*," has a strong tendency to be mastered by our possessions, and let God have second place. For when money is master, when Mammon calls the tune, whatever we may profess with our lips, we are no longer worshipping God.

It's a question of the chain of command. If I take my orders from Mammon, which means letting my decisions be regularly ruled by the motive of personal financial gain, then inevitably I shall try to make God my servant. Those who worship Mammon are always tempted to try to manipulate religion. In the book of the Acts we read of a man called Simon who dealt in magical arts, and had made a good business trading upon popular superstitions. When he came across Peter and John on one of their preaching missions, and realized that a tremendous new spiritual power was given to the Christian converts in answer to their prayers, he saw a good chance to extend his powers. The scene is vigorously depicted in the Bible, and the translation of J. B. Phillips brings out the flavor of the original. "When Simon saw how the Spirit was given through the apostles laying their hands upon people, he offered them money with the words: 'Give me this power, so that if I were to put my hands on anyone he could receive the Holy Spirit.' But Peter said to him, 'To hell with you and your money! How dare you think you could buy the gift of God?' "

This is the constant danger of Mammon worship — that we begin to think we can manipulate religion, buy off God, and thus make him our servant. Where money rules every human value is threatened, and every religious instinct perverted. Dr. Johnson once wrote: "There are few ways in which a man can be more innocently employed than in getting money" — and there's surprising truth in that. But getting money is one thing; worshipping it is another. And the subtle transition can creep upon us. Once the legitimate getting of money is transformed into a consuming passion then Mammon rules, and everything else — religion included — is enslaved. Mammon as master exacts his price: and his price is often ruined health, disrupted friendships, broken homes, and secret misery.

Now let's reverse the chain of command. What our Lord proposes to us is God as master and money as servant. The positive things he suggests about money are at least as important as the negative. Too often we have thought of his teaching solely in terms of warnings against the worship of wealth. I repeat that in his eyes money is neutral. It is for us to decide whether it will be master or servant. It makes a new stage in our Christian discipleship when we realize the amazing potential of money as the servant of the people of God. For many Christians today money is still something not to be mentioned in connection with religion. They think of Mammon as something to be forgotten when we bow in prayer. It is a revelation for many when the teaching of the Bible about stewardship finally comes home, and they see the immense potential for good that lies in money as the servant of the servant of God. This is the chain of command: God, to whom we have pledged our total allegiance; us, to whom he has entrusted possessions in this world; and Mammon, the servant who can be dispatched on the Lord's business in every direction.

It is in this light that I would like you to see your

church's budget and your part in it. If all we are concerned about is money for its own sake then we are worshipping Mammon and subtly trying to make God our servant. But if we mean what we said when we confessed our belief in "God the Father Almighty, and Jesus Christ his Son our Lord" then we are ready to catch the vision of Mammon as the servant of the church of Christ. Our Lord had a strange saying in another context about "making friends with Mammon" and I believe this is what he meant. To make friends with Mammon is so to use our money that it promotes the purposes of God, and extends his kingdom in this world.

There is all the difference in the world between thinking of money as a regrettable necessity for the maintenance of the Christian church, and money as a servant to be sent on God's business, as an instrument for his healing mission among men. Once we catch the vision of Mammon as a huge potential to be rescued from the service of self and sent on the errands of Christ we shall have an entirely different attitude to the so-called financial appeals of the church. I honestly believe that if all our members saw both their obligation and their opportunity in this light no special appeal would ever be necessary. We would all see that our dedication to Christ's cause *implies* that a proportion of our money, that extension of the self that is so dedicated, be directed to the service of his church; and we would all see that Mammon as our servant in the name of Christ can be an immense force in rescuing our city, the nation, and the world from the evils that beset us, and in bringing the healing gospel of Christ to our neighbors near and far. Have you ever thought that when in our intercessions here we pray for peace, for justice, for the healing of sick minds and bodies, for the Christian education of children, for the guidance of youth, for the care of the aged, that God may be saying to us: "Yes, I hear your prayers and will respond with my grace; but what about that servant through whom so much of what you pray for can happen, that money which is yours to give or to withhold? Mammon can speed to answer your prayers — you have only to give him the word."

Think for a moment of the ways this servant is now

being used — good, bad, and indifferent. There are good and necessary causes that absorb huge quantities of money; but there are also evil causes that command the services of Mammon without stint. And who can deny that there is in our society a vast drain on the potential of money in the service of the trivial, the tawdry, and the totally unnecessary. Are you content that money should dribble from our pockets carelessly and uselessly, that Mammon should be an unruly and unprofitable servant? The alert church member is one who says: "I'm going to bring this Mammon to heel. I'm going to decide what he shall do. And part of that decision is to mark off a serious portion of my money, and send it joyfully away out into the world in the service of Christ my Lord."

We have sounded a church alert because we believe that in a fast-moving and threatening world there is no room for a sleepy, half-hearted, conventional community of Christians. The following-through in action of the many ideas that have already sprung up from among its members will demand resources. If we have the vision of what Mammon can do, flung in as the servant of God's purposes in our own cities, in the trouble spots of our land, and in the worldwide battle for the souls of men, we shall be in no doubt as to what an alert Christian is bound to do.

There is a plain *obligation* here, but this obligation cannot be fulfilled only in words. A real church needs real support, not token contributions. I imagine that every church member would violently repudiate the idea that he considered the church of Jesus Christ as a triviality. But it is possible to indicate just that by what we give for its support in comparison with what we spend on really trivial things. The alert Christian is one who assumes a real obligation, who asks himself real questions, such as the real proportion of his income he will dispatch as the servant of the church, the real effect of inflation on the church's budget, the real facts behind the figures for its Missions and Benevolences. And the alert church member will make a pledge — not as a binding promise extracted under moral pressure, but as a statement of serious intent in fulfillment of his obligation to make Mammon the servant of God.

But I would end this sermon on another note — not obligation but *opportunity.* On all sides we are told of the difficult situation now confronting churches in large cities. I needn't list the factors that make intelligent observers skeptical about their future. I believe that this crisis is our opportunity.

Such a challenge always has been for the Christian church. Because of current skepticism it must announce its convictions in a clear voice. Because of the growth of special social problems around us it must try new ways to meet them. Because of the secularism and apathy around it, it must try to make its worship and its activities more vigorous and more real. Because of the worldwide struggle with forces of violence and division we want to reinforce our support of the mission of the church. This is our opportunity. To a large extent how we seize it will be indicated by our conscription of Mammon in the service of Christ — in plain words by our backing our beliefs with our gifts.

26. *How Fragile Is Our Faith?*

But we have this treasure in earthen vessels, that the excellency of the power may be of God, and not of us. II CORINTHIANS 4:7

I would like to think with you now about a question that bothers every sincere church member, and a great many every Sunday. It concerns the difference between the content of the Christian faith as it is set forth in the Bible and the church, and the fraction of it that we have really made our own. Is there anyone here who has never felt the contrast between *the* Faith and his faith, between the resounding statements of the Creed and his own working version of it, between the official prayers of the church and the bits that really mean something to him, between the full orchestra of the church's adoration and his own little squeak of praise?

There has always been a huge gap between what a religion stands for and what its adherents manage to absorb and practice, and nowhere is this more obvious than in Christianity. And in the history of Christianity there has perhaps never been a time when men and women have been so acutely conscious of this gap. On the one hand we are aware of the heroic assertions of the creeds and the glory of our Christian heritage; on the other hand we are even more aware of the hesitancy of our belief and the shabbiness of our Christian practice. Sunday after Sunday we are exposed to the blazing affirmations of the Bible, and share in hymns that celebrate the faith of our fathers. We confess our belief in "God the Father Almighty, maker of heaven and earth, and in Jesus Christ his only Son our Lord." We baptize babies who may one day commute to the moon in the name of one who never travelled outside a little country about the size of Connecticut, declaring that he is Lord of all time and space. We gather at the Communion table, proclaiming that Christ himself is present, uniting us to him in his resurrection power — a far greater marvel than anything made possible by modern science. We sing of a Hebrew child born two thousand years ago:

The Brightness of glory, Light of light eternal,
Our lowly nature he hath not abhorred:
Son of the Father, Word of God incarnate,
O come let us adore him, Christ the Lord.

Yet all the time we know that there is a huge gap between this Faith (with a capital F) and the faith (with a small f) that is really live in our hearts, between the traditional belief of the church and the portion of it that is a sure and certain ingredient in our everyday thinking.

Here is a "credibility gap" more important than the one that bothers the journalists in Washington. For this affects the vitality of everyone who goes by the name of "Christian," and the future of religion in the days ahead. If the gap gets wider, if we reach a point where there is very little left in common between the historic declarations of the gospel and what we really believe, then the church in this section of the world will either dwindle and die, or else be transformed into a social service club.

At the moment we are being offered a very tempting solution to this problem. It consists in a strenuous effort to reduce the content of the Faith, to reinterpret the historic creeds in such a way as to enhance their credibility for modern man. This means, in effect, saying to the bewildered believer or the die-hard doubter: "The Christian faith is not as impossible to accept as you think it is. Once we have stripped away the old clothes in which it was dressed, the foreign languages, the outmoded philosophies, the unnecessary miracles, the primitive superstitions, you will find that the credibility gap has disappeared, and it is all perfectly acceptable to reasonable people." The exponents of this view can point to the fact that there has been a great deal of misconception as to what the church considers essential beliefs, and as to what is really meant by such doctrines as creation and incarnation. It is quite true that the gap has often been made unnecessarily large by those who insist on a literal interpretation of the imagery of the Bible, and allow no room for symbolism in the creeds. Before we despair of ever being able to assent to the historic Faith we should try to insure that we know what it really is.

Yet there are surely limits to what can honestly be done to bring the Faith within the reach of every skeptical mind; and I believe that these limits are now being passed. The so-called radical theologies of today are not simply restating historic convictions in modern terms. They are gradually eliminating every belief that the world has known as distinctively Christian since Pentecost. Surely it is clear that from the very beginning Christianity has made affirmations that are not immediately acceptable to the ordinary man. St. Paul declared that the gospel in his day was a stumbling-block to the Jew and foolishness to the Greeks. The "Jew," in this context, means the naturally religious man, and the "Greek" the intellectual. Why should we expect that religious people today should not find a stumbling-block in the gospel, or that the intellectual will not continue to think of it as foolish? I see no real hope of renewal in a church that abandons the challenge of the historic creeds and offers an abbreviated version that requires no leap of faith at all. I see no future in the fashionable mini-theology dressed in polysyllables. Are we really dealing seriously with the credibility gap when we change "I believe in God the Father Almighty, maker of heaven and earth, and in Jesus Christ his only Son our Lord" to "I suggest the hypothesis that a relationship to the ultimate ground of our being implies a possible existential relationship with Jesus of Nazareth, duly demythologized"?

Those who are seeking to close the gap from this end in a sincere attempt to talk religious sense to the modern world should not be denounced as dangerous heretics, for we all need to be jolted into examining the things we say we believe, and God knows how poor an attempt the more orthodox have made to commend the Faith to our contemporaries. But surely we are getting enough of negation and denial in the struggle to bridge the gap. I don't believe the skeptical are impressed when the Christian sings: "Anything you can doubt, I can doubt better," or that the sincere atheist or agnostic wants to be patted on the back and told that he is really a good Christian all the time.

The advocates of this mini-theology are apt to use as their motto the words of St. Paul that are the text of this sermon. "We have this treasure in earthen vessels." The treasure, we are told, is the gospel, the historic Faith. Agreed. This is how the apostle sums it up in the preceding sentence: "The same God who said, 'Out of darkness let light shine,' has caused his light to shine within us, to give the light of revelation — the revelation of the glory of God in the face of Jesus Christ." The treasure is this unique and astonishing revelation of the creative God *within us* in the face of Jesus Christ. Then, we are told, the "vessels" are the creeds and confessions of the church. They are earthen vessels — and therefore, we are led to suppose, disposable. So the argument is, as Bishop Pike expounds it in his *A Time for Christian Candor,* that many traditional doctrines, such as the Holy Trinity, are earthen vessels we may cheerfully discard. The treasure remains — now held, presumably, in some shining aluminum container of the mid-twentieth century.

With all respect and affection for Bishop Pike I must protest that St. Paul says nothing of the sort. He is not talking about creeds and confessions, or any other containers of the faith — except human beings like you and me. It is perfectly plain what the "earthen vessels" are. *We* are the "earthen vessels." The New English Bible makes it even plainer. "We are no better than pots of earthenware to contain this treasure." The apostle goes on to talk of the weakness of the Christian, including himself, of our frailty, our vulnerability, our bewilderment. The treasure is still there — the amazing revelation of God in Christ — but it has been confided to the frailest of containers, the soul of people like you and me.

This is a more radical statement of the situation than offered by any reductionist theology. For this is a recognition of the gap between *the* Faith and our faith, not an attempt to cover it over. Here, right in apostolic times, it is plainly declared that there *is* a huge contrast between the revelation of God in Christ and our weak and limited apprehension of it. "We have this treasure in earthen vessels." Once we really understand this we are delivered from that nagging worry that we should be clear-eyed, confident Christians who know all the answers. Sometimes people confess to me that they are held back from church membership, or from accepting office, or even from happy participation in the services of the church, by the knowledge that their faith is very weak, that they have difficulty not only in believing all that is proclaimed but in putting into practice what they have accepted. I try to explain that this is a built-in condition of true Christianity. We are earthen vessels, and will remain so throughout this mortal life. If St. Paul felt that way, is it likely that you or I would be exempt?

If we let this text sink in we shall also be preserved from the self-assurance and arrogance with which the orthodox have sometimes assailed the heretics and doubters. I have indicated that I do not believe in the mini-theology of doubts and denials. But I hope I can avoid the worse pitfalls of a hard-baked, know-all dogmatism. If we remember that we are earthen vessels we shall not be likely to feel that unto us has been granted a monopoly of Christian truth. We shall reach that position of humility and teachableness that is the condition of spiritual growth, and the great essential if the Christian church is going to regain in days ahead the unity for which the Savior prayed.

How then does the gap look when we accept the fact that we are earthen vessels? Wider than ever — and yet with a glorious glimmer of hope. For we are now turning our eyes away from the human end of the dilemma and concentrating on the treasure we have been given. Who wants to look at an earthenware pot when its contents are glowing and sparkling before our eyes? "The same God who said, 'Out of darkness let light shine,' has caused his light to shine within us, to give the light of revelation — the revelation of the glory of God in the face of Jesus Christ." When I hear these words I know that this is true, that this is the gospel that came to me in baptism, that flickered around my childhood days, that was obscured in adolescence, that flamed again in certain crises of my life, that sustains me through these working years, and that will be my final hope when earthly days are over. The creative God, still alive, still at work, still bringing light out of darkness, the redeeming Christ still shining into our hearts the reflection of God's glory — that is what matters, not the frailty of our faith, the ups and downs of spiritual fervor. This is the real point of our text — to divert our attention from our own weak grasp to the gospel we are grasping. "We are no better than pots of earthenware to contain this treasure, *and this proves* that such transcendent power does not come from us, but is God's alone."

When we know that we are earthen vessels we have a new attitude to the credibility gap. We shall neither close our eyes and say "I *do* believe, I will believe," pushing all our doubts aside; nor will we revel in our doubts, or try to reduce the treasure to the level of our own poor understanding. We shall live by that portion of the treasure that is genuinely ours. We shall assume that there is much more that may be given us. We shall live by what we have, while looking for a fuller measure of that "transcendent power." We shall pray: "Lord, I believe; help thou mine unbelief."

The infant in arms receiving Holy Baptism among us is the prototype of the Christian. There we see ourselves, in our frailty and our weakness. What is more fragile and helpless than a human child? "Yes," said Jesus, "this is how you receive the kingdom of God." And the emphasis in baptism is not on the earthen vessel of our humanity, but on the treasure that is represented by the water — the grace of the Lord Jesus Christ, and the love of God, and the communion of the Holy Spirit. We all believe that the reality of faith, the practice of Christianity, is still to come for the infant who receives this sacrament. The God who has shined in him the light of his glory in the face of Jesus Christ, will dawn on him with increasing power and reality as the baptismal promise is fulfilled. But do we believe that this is our case now, that we are children in faith to whom so much is still to be revealed?

"We have this treasure." Let there be no doubt about that. It comes to us in Scripture, in sacrament, in the creeds and worship of the church. It cannot be identified with any other treasure in this secular world, for it comes from the world of God. It cannot be reduced to something less divine, less mysterious. It is there. We have this treasure. But we have it "in earthen vessels." If we think of our faith as contained in some impermeable casket of gleaming gold, then this text has nothing to say to us. But when we frankly confess our frailty, our inadequacy, then the grace of God can flow in, and more and more of *the* Faith will become our faith.

It's the grace of God, and not any sophistication of ours that will close the credibility gap. And perhaps the image of the "pot of earthenware" will help us to understand how it may be received. Kierkegaard uses in one of his sermons this symbol of the vessel of the soul, the cup that is waiting to be filled. He suggests that often we have turned it upside down. The grace of God pours over it but nothing is received. Could it be that we have lost the vividness of belief, missed the glory of the gospel, widened the gap between us and the faith of our fathers, because something like this has happened? What better celebration of Christmas could we look for, what surer way to renewal of our faith, and the faith of our church, than what is suggested by the reversal of this cup? The earthenware vessel will still be fragile, will still be vulnerable in the storms that are to come, but at least it will be open to what God has to bestow — the revelation of his glory in the face of Jesus Christ. Then we shall be able to make our own all that the apostle had to say. "We are no better than earthenware pots to contain this treasure, and this proves that such transcendent power does not come from us, but is God's alone. Hard-pressed on every side, we are never hemmed in; bewildered, we are never at our wit's end; hunted, we are never abandoned to our fate; struck down, we are not left to die." And we shall know what the Psalmist meant with the simple words: "My cup runneth over."

27. *The Very Idea*

Not long ago somebody asked me a question that gave me the idea for this sermon. The question was: "Where do you get your ideas for sermons?"

I began to think. Where do I get the ideas? Where does anyone get an idea? You can't just whistle them up when you want them, can you? For the last few weeks you may have been looking for an idea for a Christmas present. You looked at catalogues, at colored advertisements; perhaps you even read an article called "Ideas for Christmas." But the idea wouldn't come. Then when you were doing something else, like washing the dishes, or reading the newspaper, or listening to a sermon, suddenly the idea popped into your mind, and you said to yourself: "That's it: the very idea." And so someone this Christmas morning opened a parcel, unwrapped your gift, and said: "What a fascinating present. Where did you get the idea?"

Everybody here — from the youngest to the oldest — knows what an idea is, but nobody has ever seen one. There are billions of ideas floating around in the world at this very moment but nobody knows how to catch them. Every now and then, for no particular reason, one of them jumps up through a trapdoor in someone's mind and he says: "I've got an idea!" Some have loose trapdoors so that ideas get in very easily: others have them so rusted and stiff to open that an idea can only get through about once a year. Then some people have a little net beside the trapdoor that lets the good ideas through, but keeps the bad ones out. Others just let them all come in — and that's where the trouble starts. For there *are* good ideas and bad ideas, just as there are big ideas and small ideas, dull ideas and crazy ideas, sleepy ideas and working ideas. And, of course, there is always the *very* idea. That's the one we really want. Other people don't always understand, but they know our very idea when we produce it. When Werner Von Braun, the expert on rockets and spaceships, was a small boy he got the idea he would like one day to send a capsule to the moon. And I'm sure when he mentioned it to his mother she said: "To the moon! The very idea!" But it was his very idea — and look what's happening now.

So there was I, walking down the street not long ago, wondering where ideas come from. If anyone had asked me I should have had to reply: "I have no idea" — and that's a terrible thing, to have no idea. So I began to daydream. All around me were the big stores twinkling with things to buy, from lollipops to diamond-studded mink coats for poodles, but not one of them had any ideas for sale. So I dreamed away off to another part of the city, where the lights were dim, and there was a little crooked street with no traffic. In the middle of it was a rickety old building, lit with candles and brass lamps. And on it was a huge sign, made of oranges and lemons, that spelled out the word: IDEA-SHOP. Underneath a long column of red ants were moving up and down, spelling out the words: GET YOUR IDEAS HERE.

So I pushed open the door. Instead of ringing a bell it set off a kind of twang inside me, just like what happens when you feel an idea coming. And sure enough there were the ideas. They were floating all over the place and bounding against the roof — like toy balloons. "Can I help you?" said a little squeaky voice, and there was a little old man with a long white beard. "I want an idea," I said. "You've come to the right place," he replied, "I'm the idea-merchant. What kind of an idea do you want? Would you like a brilliant idea, or a stupid idea? a lovely idea or a horrid idea? a wonderful idea or a miserable idea? I've got them all." And sure enough there were all the ideas drifting around the shop — red ones, blue ones, grey ones, green ones, yellow ones, and many-colored ones. "I want a good idea," I said, "for a sermon." He looked puzzled. "I'm not often asked for these: they usually go to our secondhand department. But have a look around." I pointed to a brilliant crimson balloon and asked, "Is that a good idea?" "I can't tell you," he said, "no one can tell which are the good ideas and which are the bad in here. You have to try them out." That seemed funny, and yet somehow reasonable enough. Then I noticed a heap in the corner of dull lead-colored balloons that were not moving at all. "I sell lots of these," the old man said; "people say they cause less trouble than any others. They never get off the ground." I turned away from the lead balloons and noticed a little doorway in the back of the shop, gleaming with gold and encrusted with precious stones. "What's in there?" I asked. "I think I'd like the idea you keep hidden away behind that lovely door." "I'm sure you would," he answered, "that's where we keep the Very Idea." "But that's the very one I want!" I shouted. "Let me in there at once — and you can keep all the others." He shook his head. "No: the only way is to stay here all day, and perhaps all night, and perhaps all tomorrow. Then when all the other ideas have danced around you for long enough that door will just open — and the Very Idea will be yours."

The very thought of waiting so long woke me up from my daydream, and there I was — stepping off the sidewalk on that street against the red lights. And a taxi-driver leaned out and said: "Hi! mister; what's the big idea?" I was just about to tell him, when I realized he wouldn't understand. But somewhere in the back of my mind an idea was already there.

A few days later I was reading the Bible, reading the very passage on which this sermon is based. At Christmas we always read from the opening chapters of the Gospels, for that is where we hear about the coming of Jesus Christ to our world. But you must have noticed that the opening verses of the Fourth Gospel are very different from the others. In fact, they are so different that some of you may have wondered what they mean, and what they have to do with the birth of Jesus. Yet these are some of the most exciting and wonderful words ever written. The man who wrote them knew that we have the story about Mary and Joseph, about the shepherds and the wise men, and about the birth of the baby Jesus in a stable, in St. Matthew and St. Luke. So he wanted to tell us more, to thrill us with the deep, deep meaning of what happened at Bethlehem, and all that went before. In the other Gospels we have the story like a pure and simple little tune on the piano. In this Gospel a great orchestra picks up the tune, and transports us in through time and eternity in a great symphony of mystery and love. What it says we will never fully understand, but I don't believe there is anyone here too young to hear the exciting things that are being said. This is not a fairytale or a daydream. It is God's answer to the questions that all of us have asked from the time we were very small.

"In the beginning. . . ." Every one of us asks about beginnings. Where did I come from? My parents; then where did they come from? and their parents; and their parents; and their parents — right back to — what? And where did the world come from? From this solar system wheeling around the sun? And where did it come from? From some galaxy in space? And where did that come from? And the other galaxies that came before it, away, back, back into endless time. How did it all begin? Well, these three words, like the same three words in the book of Genesis, take us right back to the very beginning. The opening four words of the Bible are: "In the beginning, God. . . ." And when you say "God," you have got to the beginning. You can't think any farther back; for this is part of what God means. Full stop; he IS the beginning.

Do you think God must have been lonely when there was no one and nothing else at all? Just God. In the beginning. God — and nothing, nothing, nothing. But listen again. It wasn't like that. God was not alone; not even in the beginning. "In the beginning," says this Gospel, "was the Word, and the Word was with God, and the Word was God." If you find that hard to understand, how about this? "In the beginning was the Idea." This is what it means. God was not lonely, because he had an Idea. And, of course, it was a good Idea, and a working Idea. God has no bad ideas, and God has no sleepy ideas. They are all good and they all work. And what was his Idea? It was to create — to make something. You know what it is to have an idea of creation, don't you? The idea comes — to make a drawing, or a garden, or a poem, or a model airplane, or a Christmas present for a friend. Creative ideas are the best ideas — for they make something happen. That's how it was with God's Idea. He made things happen. A universe came into being — first perhaps just a little energy; then something like a ball of gas; then something solid; then stars and suns and moons; then little corners of this huge universe where things began to grow, where life appeared, plants and trees and vegetables; fishes and reptiles and great beasts of the forest. This was what God's Idea — God's Word — did. "All things were made by him, and without him was not anything made that was made." "And God saw everything that he had made, and, behold, it was very good."

So there was a whole universe, a wonder of light and motion and energy, and in it there were also spirits of God's creation, invisible angels to celebrate his glory. It was, if you like, a swinging universe, where, as the Bible says, "the morning stars sang together, and all the sons of God shouted for joy."

Then God's Idea got to work again; and in one little corner where life was growing very fast, he slowly brought into being a new creature called Man. God's Idea was that there should be on this little planet someone who could be like a son to him, able to talk with him, able to work with him, and able to create things too. He didn't just want a lot of things. He wanted a family, sons and daughters he would love, and who could love him. So the human family came into being.

But, as you know, sons and daughters are not like stars and planets. They do not always do what they are told. God's Idea was love — that they should love him and love one another. But soon God's family had another idea — a bad idea. (Don't ask me where the bad ideas come from: nobody really knows.) The bad idea was to say No to the Father-God, to disobey him, and to refuse to love him. This is the sad part of the story. For soon men and women got more and more bad ideas — in fact one led to another. When they stopped loving God they stopped loving one another. They began to hate, to fear, to quarrel, and even to kill. God's good Idea was still there but most of the time men and women were refusing it. They were his family but they didn't really want him. "He came unto his own, and his own received him not." They followed the bad idea. The good Idea was still shining away in the darkness, but only a few really paid attention. They were his true sons and daughters. "As many as received him to them gave he power to become sons of God."

What could God do when he saw so many following the bad ideas, so that the earth was full of fears and suspicion, wars, plagues, violence, and misery? He could have let his family go: one little word and the whole planet with everybody on it could just disappear back into nothingness. Or he could have appeared to his family in a flash of heavenly fire, and a great voice like thunder, so that everyone would be terrified back to his family, and to obey the good Idea. But, since God is love, he wouldn't do either of these things. Instead he had another Idea. And when the rumor of it spread through heaven there was immense excitement. When it was whispered among the angels, they all said: "The Very Idea!" — for it was the most amazing Idea that had ever been known. God was going to meet with his family — not to destroy them and begin again, and not to terrify them into submission, but as a little child, born into a human home and delivered over to all the dangers and horrors that bad ideas had brought into the world. This time it was not just going to be an Idea that was given to man. It was the Very Idea — and that meant that God's Idea was going to become a real person, a human child such as we all have been. So, very quietly, one night two thousand years ago, when the world was busy about its affairs, in a little stable of a little town in a little country Jesus was born. St. Luke tells us that Mary his mother "brought forth her firstborn son, and wrapped him in swaddling clothes, and laid him in a manger." St. John says: "The Word — the Idea — was made flesh, and dwelt among us."

I have called Jesus God's Very Idea, because *very* means true and real. This was God's good Idea for men made true and real for us all. For no longer did men have to seek among all the bad ideas to find God's good Idea of love. Now it had become real. God's Idea had flesh and blood like us. God's love had a human face, and human eyes, and a human tongue. Now at last men could see what it really meant to be a son of God. For as Jesus grew up and mixed with all kinds of people he loved his Father all the time, and loved every man, woman and child whom he met. Then, as now, the world was full of bad ideas as well as good ones, but never could a bad idea get in through that trapdoor into his mind or heart. Even when the bad ideas swarmed around him, even when the very worst idea that ever was got into the minds of men, and they hung him on a cross, still he went on loving them and loving his Father in Heaven. "Father," he said from that cross, "forgive them, for they know not what they do." But men could not kill God's Idea. Jesus came alive again and is still in our world, still the Very Idea of God, still the one who puts the good ideas into our minds and drives the bad ideas away.

Have you ever noticed that for the few days around Christmas in our homes, in the streets and the shops, in the city, in the nation, and even in the struggles between nations, there are more good ideas around, and fewer bad ones? There's just a little more love, isn't there? and a little less hate? a little more caring for others, and a little less selfishness? a little more understanding, and a little less violence? a little less strife and a little more peace? We come to worship on Christmas Day because like the first disciples we behold his glory. But to behold his glory doesn't mean just to sing carols and praise the name of Jesus. It means to reflect his love, to put the good ideas he gives us into action. If we listen to the story of Jesus in church good ideas will come. But if, outside the church, we begin to love people we don't like, to spend more on other people and less on ourselves, to say things that help and never things that hurt, to be unselfish in our decisions and kind in our judgments, then we will really know what Christmas means. For that is the Very Idea.

28. *Churches in Turmoil*

But now we are discharged from the law, dead to that which held us captive, so that we serve not under the old written code but in the new life of the Spirit.

ROMANS 7:6 (RSV)

Shortly before Christmas 1966 the people of Britain were startled to read in the newspapers that Dr. Charles Davis, the nation's leading Roman Catholic theologian, had announced that he was quitting the priesthood and severing his connection with the church. He stated frankly that he could no longer accept the doctrines of papal infallibility and primacy, and indicated his dissatisfaction with the church as an institution in the modern world. Dr. Davis was one of the "periti" — theological experts — at the Vatican Council, and was about to leave for Italy for an important conference between Roman Catholics and Anglicans when this dramatic decision was made. The shock of this public defection has extended far beyond the British Isles and there has been inevitable speculation as to how many others may be on the edge of a similar decision.

Fifty — or even ten — years ago such an event would have been hailed by Protestants with considerable satisfaction, if not actual glee. It would have been scored up against notable conversions to the Roman Church such as that of John Henry Newman. He would have been triumphally welcomed into the Protestant fold as one whose eyes had been opened to the errors of Rome. It is a sign of our times that there has been no such reaction from responsible Protestants in Britain today nor — if we have any sense — will there be from any of us. In a world where the entire Christian church is under heavy attack there is no room for the lunacies of sectarian rivalry. We have still serious differences with our Roman brethren, but only those who are blind to the worldwide crisis of Christianity and deaf to the ecumenical spirit of our age could derive any satisfaction from the defection of Dr. Davis. His sincere and moving statement does not simply call in question such doctrines as papal infallibility. That we would welcome. It goes much farther. It throws a penetrating and skeptical light on the entire institution of the church in whatever form it exists today. It is not just the Vatican that has to respond to the challenge of this defection. It is every organized Christian institution in the world.

For what does he say? "The church is now breaking up and some other form of Christian presence in the world is under formation." These are not the words of a man simply switching allegiance within the Christian fold. They express the turmoil that is agitating every corner of Christendom today. You can sense it in every land, and in every denomination. It can most simply be described as a revolt against the system. Everywhere there are signs of restlessness. Systems of belief, systems of church government, systems of public worship — all are being vigorously questioned. It is as though the churches were beginning to agree with their critics that organized religion, in any form, is out of tune with the spirit of the age. What Dr. Davis is saying is not just that he finds the Roman Church too rigid and slow-moving, but that churches of any kind as we know them today have outlived their usefulness, and that Christianity will have to be expressed in the modern world in a completely new way. "The church is now breaking up."

Is this true? I think you know that I have little sympathy with the flood of negative criticism of the churches that flows from ivory towers, and even less for those who claim that the only way forward lies through a repudiation of the basic doctrines of the creeds. But I hope never to be guilty of the false prophecy which says: "Peace, peace: where there is no peace." We can't sit here congratulating ourselves that we have a lively church, that our organization is ticking over, our expanding budgets met, and that we are part of a huge, expanding denomination — as if there were no real crisis in the church today. We can't forget the immense defection from the Christian ranks throughout the world. We can't close our eyes to the minimal impact the churches make in our city. We can't be deaf to the rumblings of doubt and disbelief that sound in the courts and councils and seminaries, or the cynical judgment that "the church has had it." We can't ignore the host of people of goodwill who claim to be religious but recoil from its organized expression, those who desperately want the spirit of Christianity but reject its systems.

The churches *are* in turmoil. We are living through a period of upheaval perhaps more critical than the church has ever known before. And we shall live it through as *Christians* — not as Presbyterians, Anglicans, Roman Catholics, or Baptists. For the one great question before us has little to do with our denominational squabbles. It concerns the life or death of the Christian church as a recognizable community in the world ahead of us. And it can be put like this: Does the present turmoil of the churches presage reformation or decay? If there is a breakup, or breakdown, of traditional systems going on in the church today, if there is a fundamental questioning of standard beliefs and practices, if there is an accelerating decline in the authority of all religious institutions, does this mean the renewal or the dissolution of the church as we know it? Are we watching the slow demise of a venerable religious system, or are we on the edge of a new Reformation?

The answer to this question lies, I believe, in the response of the church — and by the church I don't mean here the World Council of Churches, or the Vatican, but you and me — to the presence and power of the Spirit of God. If that sounds like conventional verbiage it's because we have really ceased to believe in an active, renovating, awakening divine Spirit in the life of men and nations. According to the Bible the Holy Spirit is God in action now, God at work in his world, God changing human lives, God directing his people into new ways and new discoveries. And the Bible records again and again how in a time of chaos and dissolution the Spirit breathes new life into the systems of man's creation. Genesis records that when "the earth was without form and void; and darkness was upon the face of the deep, the Spirit of God moved upon the face of the waters." Jeremiah, who was driven to despair by the breakdown of the religious systems of his day and the ineffectiveness of the traditional laws, had the courage to proclaim a new day when God's Spirit would bring new life to his people. "After those days, saith the Lord, I will put my law in their inmost parts, and write it in their hearts; and will be their God, and they shall be my people." Ezekiel, seeing the religious systems of his time as a valley of dry bones, and hearing the question, "Can these bones live?" is impelled to prophesy: "Thus saith the Lord God: 'Come from the four winds, O breath, and breathe upon these slain that they may live.' And the breath came into them, and they lived, and stood up upon their feet, an exceeding great army."

So, our Lord when he delivered his first sermon to a people who were living in a frozen system of religious law in a world of cynicism and despair, opened with the words: "The Spirit of the Lord is upon me, because he hath anointed me to preach the gospel to the poor; he hath sent me to heal the broken-hearted, to preach deliverance to the captives, and recovering of sight to the blind, to set at liberty them that are bruised."

And so St. Paul, when he found the infant church — alone and afraid in a world of brutality and license — beginning to clutch again the written codes, the system from which they had been set free, wrote these words of our text: "But now we are discharged from the law, dead to that which held us captive, so that we serve not under the old written code but in the new life of the Spirit."

"Not under the old written code but in the new life of the Spirit." St. Paul is here referring to the contrast between living under the Old Testament laws and living in free response to the Spirit of Christ. The Law of God, as a revelation of his will, was the heart and center of the covenant of the Lord with his people; but it had over the centuries tended to harden into a rigid system of religion. The written code had become an institution that controlled every aspect of life, an institution that could not be reformed. The religious establishment, with its codes and ceremonies, came to be regarded as sacrosanct, to be revered and obeyed even at the expense of human needs — almost in the place of God. It was this system with which our Lord collided on more than one occasion. He saw how, for instance, a rigid interpretation of the Sabbath laws could make religious men totally indifferent to the real inner meaning of God's laws and to the instincts of compassion. So, when he found objections being raised to such trivialities as his disciples' plucking ears of corn on the Sabbath day, or to his healing a man with a withered arm, he was distressed and angry. This was the time when he announced the principle that destroys all system worship, religious or secular, then and now. "The Sabbath was made for the sake of man and not man for the Sabbath." That goes for every system that was ever devised. The church was made for the sake of man, not man for the church. The state was made for the sake of man, not man for the state. It is in this sense that we have to hear the words "We serve not under the old written code, but in the new life of the Spirit."

Does this mean, then, that all church-systems, all religious establishments are deadly, and that we should really rejoice at the possibility of the breakup of the church? There are some who seem to feel that this is the only answer. They contrast the deadening effect of all systems — creeds, organized worship, the structure of local organizations, the offices and officials of the church — with the life-giving impulse of a free spontaneous faith. This is particularly attractive to this generation that suffers from the power of the institution and the overorganization of all aspects of life. There are millions around us who say: "I have enough systems around me to choke the spirit out of me. Don't give me a religious system on top of everything else. I want to worship God in my own way. I want to be a Christian without another establishment around my neck." And so the turmoil in the churches throws up the notion that the time has come for Christianity to be present in our world in some more spontaneous and liberating way than is represented by the churches as we know them.

I find it impossible to justify this extreme view either from the evidence of Scripture or the record of the church. There is no trace in the Bible of a merely individual religion. The covenants, both old and new, are made with a community — the "People of God." And where you have a community you inevitably have some kind of a system. It cannot be avoided. Suppose a group of members of your church decided they had had enough of organized religion as they found it there and left that community in order to try to find a more real and vital expression of worship and service. They might have much to be said on their side: they might have the very best motives; they might sincerely seek the freedom of the Spirit. But one thing is certain. Whatever new ways of worship they might devise, whatever close fellowship they might discover, whatever Christian action they might decide to do, sooner or later they would have a system, a new establishment. Again and again this has happened in the course of Christian history. The most revolutionary breakaways, such as that of the Methodists or even of the Society of Friends, have always led to the creation of yet another system, a different kind of establishment.

Let it be said: system itself is not wrong; some form of establishment is inevitable whenever two or three people get together to do anything at all. When Dr. Davis was asked what new form of Christian presence in the world he had in mind he said he did not know, except that it would be more informal and flexible. He was too good a church historian not to know that some system would inevitably appear.

We cannot therefore just pose the simple choice: system versus Spirit. Our Lord himself did not imply on any occasion that he totally rejected the religious establishment of his day. We remember the occasions on which he opposed it in the name of the Spirit of God; but we tend to forget his loyalty to the organized religion in which he was raised. He went regularly to the Sabbath services; he studied the Law; he respected the precepts of Judaism. So completely did he accept the system that his disciples never thought of leaving the religion of the synagogue till they were forced out. St. Paul not only honored the system of his fathers, but when the church developed its own system of worship and discipline he upheld it to the limit of his extensive vocabulary. Those who wanted to break up the church and live in a kind of individual freedom of the Spirit he didn't hesitate to call "dogs and evil-workers." What church history reveals is not that system itself is the evil, but that unless it is constantly exposed to the life-giving Spirit it tends to petrify and to corrupt.

As Christians we are within the system, but we don't live by it. "We serve not under the old written code but in the new life of the Spirit." To abandon the code, to wreck the establishment, is the way to dissolution. To maintain the system, but to reform it from within is the way to renewal and newness of life.

Let me apply that to our own situation. Suppose we listened to the siren voices that tell us the day of the church-on-the-corner is over, and simply abolish this church. Do you think that would really lead to new life? Some might indeed find an invigoration and a challenge — and then, like the hypothetical group I mentioned before, would develop their own new system. But my guess is that if this happened to every parish church in the land, chances of Christianity's surviving as a living force would be slim indeed. It is not just the witness of public worship and proclamation of the gospel that would disappear. It would also be the vast silent work of pastoral care and responsibility for our brethren across the world that would be lost.

This is not to say that the system under which we work and worship is sacrosanct and unchangeable. On the contrary it is certain that changes — perhaps great changes — must be made in the form of our Christian presence in our own city. Such changes involve experiments — and experiments involve mistakes. I hope we shall be a church that is not afraid to change, and not afraid to risk mistake. "We serve not under the old written code" — yet there is always a tendency to worship that old written code, to complain if things are not done exactly as they were ten, twenty, or fifty years ago. If we are to serve "in the new life of the Spirit" we must be alert to what that Spirit is saying to us today. Our task is not to abolish the systems we have inherited, or to lose patience with the sometimes clumsy machinery of the church, but to seek that power and presence that alone can renew our life as a community of Christ.

I have spoken much about the church as an institution in this message. But the real church, of course, is not an establishment or a system. It is people — it is you and I. And you and I also know in our own souls what St. Paul means when he says: "We serve not under the old written code but in the new life of the Spirit." As he put it elsewhere: "the letter killeth, but the spirit giveth life." Do you never feel that your religion is throttling you, that the system of prayers, the habits of worship, the beliefs you profess, are a kind of dead weight that you would gladly dump if you dared? Probably more of us than you think have had such thoughts. The answer, again, is not to let the system go, to cut loose in the hope of finding some private faith to sustain you. Whenever that temptation comes somewhere you will hear an echo of that haunting question of Christ to his disciples: "Will you also go away?" and deep down you will have to reply as they did: "Lord, to whom shall we go? Thou hast the words of eternal life." No: the answer is "the new life of the Spirit." To be alert to the Spirit, to know that God is alive as a presence and a power, is to experience how your religion can come alive again, your prayers take on new meaning, your church membership tingle with a new meaning and possibilities. If there is any breaking up going on in the church, in our own souls, let it not be the preface to dissolution, but to that newness of life that the Spirit is waiting to bring at the very moment the waters are stirred.